I0108921

Tales of a Cycling Nomad 1982

3,500 Miles on a Bike

Dave Simon

www.ten16press.com - Waukesha, WI

Tales of a Cycling Nomad 1982: 3,500 Miles on a Bike

ISBN 978-1-948365-33-8
Second Edition

Tales of a Cycling Nomad 1982: 3,500 Miles on a Bike
by Dave Simon

For information, please contact:

www.ten16press.com
Waukesha, WI

Edited by Lauren Blue
Map creation by Therese Joanis

This book is dedicated to my older brother Peter, who made it happen. His encouragement and belief in the stories captured in this book got me off my butt and tapping the keyboard to paint the picture from that summer's bicycling journey across North America. Thanks bro. I love you.

Vancouver
Bellingham
Calgary
WASHINGTON
Port Angeles
Yakima
OREGON
IDAHO
Unity
WYOMIN
Steamboat Springs
Denver
COLORADO

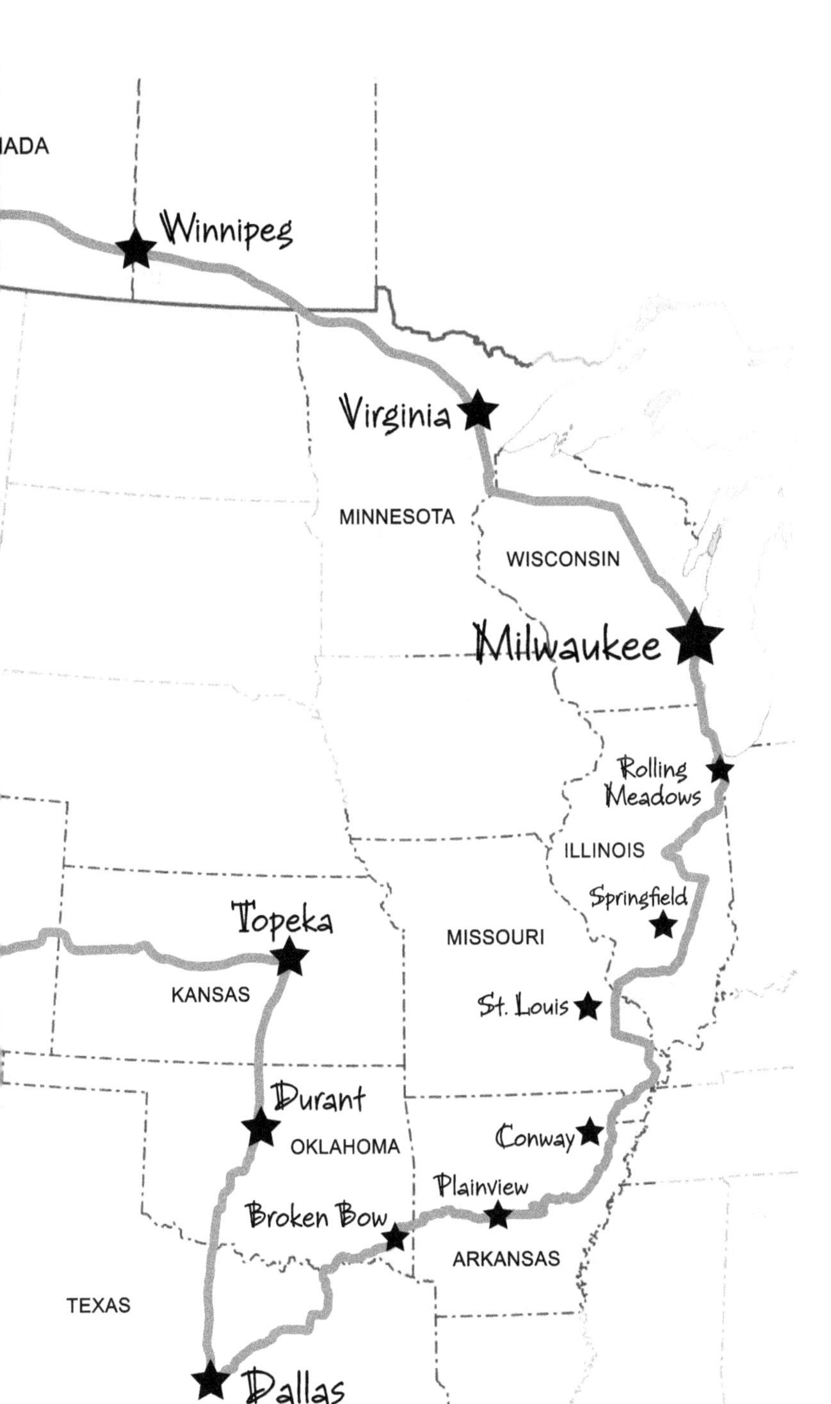
ADA
Winnipeg
Virginia
MINNESOTA
WISCONSIN
Milwaukee
Rolling Meadows
ILLINOIS
Springfield
Topeka
MISSOURI
KANSAS
St. Louis
Durant
OKLAHOMA
Conway
Plainview
Broken Bow
ARKANSAS
TEXAS
Dallas

Prologue

I'm not sure when the idea hit me. Or when it went from a "wish" to a "desire" to a "goal," but at some point, I developed a notion in my head about wanting to bicycle across America.

I've always loved bicycling, starting back in grade school tooling around on my 3-speed red Stingray with the banana seat and high handlebars. In college, it was easier and faster to get to classes on a bicycle. Once I started working full-time, I slowly took longer distance rides. They invigorated and challenged me. There was (and is) something special about being out in the fresh air, pushing yourself, discovering things without the aid of an automobile.

My older brother Peter has often asked me what motivated me to take the trip I did in 1982. The answer is not simple. It's also not necessarily profound. I wanted to explore America

Third or fourth grade

firsthand. I didn't want to do that in a car. I wanted to challenge myself on a bicycle and be outdoors, meeting people, conquering mountains, exploring wherever the whim took me for the day or week. A bicycle is perfect for that. As long as your legs hold out, you're golden. I wanted to meet new people and see parts of the country I hadn't seen before, particularly west of the Rocky Mountains and the Pacific Northwest. A bicycle was a good way to do that.

Traversing the U.S. and Canada by bike also meant saving money. Having gone back to school at the University of Wisconsin-Milwaukee when I took time off for this trip, money was not flowing into my pockets. So, the cheaper I could get around, the better. A bike is great for that.

In some ways, I knew there would be a story about the trip. During the journey, I spent a lot of time writing short stories, poetry, and essays. The account here in *Tales of a Cycling Nomad 1982* is different than what I wrote that summer. Here I capture the events and feel of the journey – agony and sweat, close encounters and scary camping, the pull of the open road and the loneliness that goes along with it.

I hope you enjoy the personal stories enough to share them with others. I've been asked by multiple friends to write down what I saw, learned, and experienced in 1982, and to the best of my recollection, I've captured that accurately here.

Dave Simon
Merton, WI
April 2018

N
W
E
S
Menomonee Falls
Milwaukee
Waukesha
Cudahy
Oak Creek
Racine
Lake Michigar
Elkhorn
Burlington
Kenosha
WISCONSIN
ILLINOIS
Antioch
Round Lake Beach
Waukegan
Woodstock
Libertyville
Crystal Lake
Lake Zurich
Highland Park
Rolling Meadows
Des Plaines
Schaumburg

Chapter 1
Leaving Milwaukee Behind

May 1, 1982. Tom Ake, Carl Lindquist, and I head to a local dive for breakfast on Oakland Avenue on Milwaukee's East Side. Our breath makes thick white plumes in the air. The temperature hovers around freezing. I'm going to stoke up for a 100-mile bike ride south as part of my first day on a four-month bicycle journey by myself across North America. Nerves, yes. Excitement, yes. Trepidation, yes.

Tom, Carl, and I work at Sentry Foods on Downer Avenue and attend UWM (University of Wisconsin-Milwaukee) with varying degrees of focus. I've spoken to my professors and have either finished up my classes early for the semester or they've allowed me to take the final when I get back at the end of the summer. They support this quest.

My older brother Peter and his wife Pat gave me a pair of pants/shorts that can be adjusted (you can shed the bottom half if it starts to get warmer). I wear these to start the day.

We eat. Goodbyes are said. I launch my bicycle loaded with bare minimal necessities (a sleeping bag, a day's worth of food, a one-person tent, a flashlight, one change of underwear, a shirt, a pair of socks, a pair of pants, two books to read, my journal, and a map of Wisconsin/Illinois).

Pre-trip haircut

There is no GPS, no smart phone, no Internet, no credit card. I have $220 in my pocket to make it four months, and I know that I will have to work at some point along the way to continue this trek. Multiple friends have donated $1, $5, $10, and $20 bills and signed them so that when I spend them, I will remember their faces and our friendship. Tom's and Seth Duhnke's, another Sentry coworker, have been stored in a special place for motivation. Their words resonate about philosophy, jazz, and the journey of life we all must choose to experience on our own, the challenges we face, the niche we carve on the planet.

The map will get me through southeast Wisconsin and into northern Illinois. I've chosen only to bring that one section with me. As I approach or cross state borders, the plan is to pick up the next map at that point. I can't get ahead of myself.

My hands are cold. There's a hazy blue to the sky, promising a warm-up. We hug, and I shove off.

The desire to hit the road, be free, explore America, see the great Pacific Northwest, and do it on two wheels fuels me. I want to see much more of this country, be face-to-face with people, put a finger on the pulse. The itch has been with me for years, starting after graduation from the University of Illinois (UofI) in 1978. Here and there I began taking longer jaunts on my bike, pushing myself, wondering how far I could go, what the next day would hold if I just continued exerting myself. What would it be like to keep pedaling away and see where I end up? The question captivates me.

The motivation grew from there. Now I've got the time to take off and not worry about a job, school, or other responsibilities. A career can wait this summer. I'm ready for the road.

***

Drivers in Wisconsin are nice, and navigating the metro area proves easy. Houses and businesses slowly fall away. Farmland, rolling hills, and open space beckon. A rhythm develops. The sun rises in the sky. I stop after 25-30 miles and take the pant legs off, leaving just the shorts on. The result feels good, like emerging from a cocoon.

I've trained for this odyssey for most of the spring. The highest mileages as part of the training regime were two 50-mile days, the bicycle loaded with most of the trip's gear. I needed to test my stamina and distance. How far would I be able to go? What would the body endure?

There were no issues then and none today. The day heats up. I finish my water and fill up (two water bottles are on the bike, one under the top of the rim and one angled up where most bicyclists place it). The extra bottle isn't needed today, but getting out to the western part of the United States, I know there will be huge distances between towns, and extra water capacity could be a potentially lifesaving measure.

I experience a mental victory crossing the border into Illinois. I'm closing in on my younger brother Kurt's apartment in what he facetiously terms Rolling Ghettos (Rolling Meadows). I navigate the two-lane highways, which slowly change to suburban streets, until I must stop to look at the map and figure out where his apartment sits.

For the first and only time that summer, I crash. My thin front tire on the 18-speed touring bike wedges between the concrete of the curb and the asphalt of the road. There was a small gap. The tire slides into it as the bike stops, and I teeter for several seconds, then crash with a string of profanity. Nothing scraped, bloodied, or broken, just a bit of my pride going south. You think you know how to ride a bike and handle yourself, and in the most mundane situation, you eat turf.

I didn't think about crashing my bike. I'm surprised when I fall, and it's a small reminder to pay attention to my surroundings. The slightest incident can become dangerous and imperil the trip. I don't want that to happen, so I file away the situation in the memory banks.

I determined before the trip, and the day's ride reinforces, that biking gloves are one of the most important pieces of equipment when you ride a bicycle a lot. Get your hands out when you fall, let the gloves take the impact. You avoid scrapes and gravel raking your hands, and you help prevent more serious injury by using your hands to break your fall.

Pizza awaits at the apartment. Kurt's buddy Greg Tamm joins us. I eat a large pizza by myself. We drink some beer. I marvel while I'm standing on his back deck looking out that I covered 100 miles on the first day. There's a buzz from the adrenaline – and the beer.

The conversation ranges all over the place. Greg is a roommate of Kurt's from UofI and is a thoughtful, funny, and iconoclastic individual. We cover everything from how bridges

First night of the trip at my brother's place

are constructed to the prospects of the Cubs in baseball. But mostly it's good to be with friends, knowing there's a comfortable bed waiting.

I'm grateful to have a place to crash the first evening. There is fear in the back of my head when I have to be totally on my own, finding a place to camp and sleep by the side of the road. Tonight brings me the comfort of family and friendship. The game plan is to stay with friends through Illinois and down to St. Louis before hopping off into the great unknown of the Ozarks on my way to Dallas. I sleep well.

First night of the trip at my brother's place

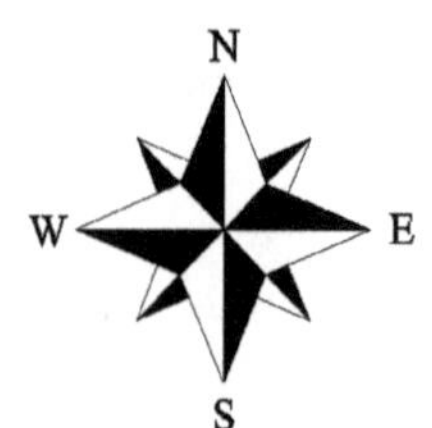
N
W
E
S

Rolling Meadows
Naperville
Joliet

Ottawa
Kankakee River State Park
Kankakee

Peoria
Bloomington

Champaign

Springfield

Chapter 2
Wind

After an uneventful ride and night over in Blue Island, days three and four of the trip take me to Naperville and Ottawa, Illinois, staying overnight with buddies Rich Brown and Jack Novotney.

I spent a lot of time with Rich and Jack while living in Ottawa from 1978-80 after graduating from UofI – playing basketball with Rich in Naperville and drinking the necessary beers and socializing afterwards. Jack was in Ottawa and helped me navigate those first years on the full-time job – getting to know people in the area, hitting the ski slopes in Wisconsin together, water skiing. Their friendship kept me going while I was in a sales job, hitting the road every week. In some ways, that period contributed to this bike trip, getting a taste of northern Illinois in a vehicle and wanting to go farther, see more, but do it slowly, experiencing the land firsthand.

It's not until I get to St. Louis that I will begin pitching my tent at the side of the road. I'm a bit nervous about that. The first week or so of staying with friends through Illinois should prep me.

One of the things you don't consider when planning a long bicycle trip like this is the wind – aiding you on some days and on others making you wonder why you're out there, kind of like life. It's an early lesson of the voyage. The wind dominates you some days, and some days you dominate because of the wind.

It's an extremely tough day biking down to Ottawa. Leaving Naperville for Ottawa, I take two-lane roads, and it's not until Norway that I start thinking, "What the heck am I doing on this bicycle?"

Prevailing winds this time of year are from the southwest. I'm biking southwest, directly into it. When I left Naperville in the morning, it didn't seem too bad. Now it's cranking in my face. Pedaling hard gets me nowhere. Frustration builds.

The land is mostly flat, with large plowed fields ready to start sprouting corn. This is Illinois farm country – black earth, very slight rolling hills, lots of nothingness towards the horizon, sprinkled with a few small towns here and there and dotted with farmhouses once you get through the tiny communities.

Norway is a small settlement, originally settled by, oddly enough, Norwegians. Not much is there – a few houses, that's about it. One of the first epiphanies of the trip emerges as I pedal past the outcrop of homes: STOP FIGHTING IT. Stop fighting the wind. Accept it. You don't have much choice. Make the most of it. If you have to stop and rest, stop and rest.

The small revelation helps me the rest of the way down Illinois Highway 71 and into Ottawa.

***

Wind continues to be an issue the next few days (as it always is in Illinois during the spring). Ottawa to Kankakee is another tough day, close to 70 miles. It's a bit ragged and gusty, but I make it safely and catch up with Dennis "Bubba" Clark and Jessica MacKinnon.

Jessica and Bubba I've known since high school, great friends who've stayed in touch. Jessica went to UofI as well, then took an editorship position in Wilmington, Illinois, where I'd often stop by on my sales job while living in Ottawa. We never solved the world's problems, but we had great discussions and certainly aired them all out. She's now working for Kankakee Community College.

Bubba is one of the greatest athletes I've known in my life, a true winner and one of the wittiest people to grace the planet. He's "Bubba" because of his size, and his personality lives up to that as well – he'll dominate a room, make friends with everyone, and win a race for mayor of Kankakee if he'd ever want the job.

Leaving Kankakee fresh and early May 5, the wind has shifted. I don't know this. I've called my friend Mike "Boud" Boudreau, who lives in Champaign, to meet later in the day and tell him how long it's going to take me – six or seven hours based on my early pilgrimage. I'm presuming my average of 12.5 mph (more or less touring speed on a bicycle) will continue. NOT!

The air is crisp. I breathe deeply through my nose and let the spring aromas sift into me. There's a bite in the air. The wind shifted overnight but that doesn't mean anything until I'm back in the saddle.

Interstate 57 leads to the University of Illinois and Champaign/Urbana from Kankakee, but you cannot bike that. I head off down I-45, a beat-up piece of crap two-lane highway, potholed and crumbling apart on the sides (you find out a LOT about the state of roads in the United States by bicycling across the country). I pop out of low gears I've been using the first four days into a higher gear. Pedaling at an easy pace, I raise my gears again.

This continues mile after mile until I've easily slipped into the highest gear on the 18-speed with relative ease and I'm pumping and pumping away, not breathing hard, not sweating. What the heck?

I'm not tired, don't need water, have no desire to stop. Yet I'm way ahead of schedule. I stop in Watseka at a gas station, enjoy the head rush, wonder why I'm going so fast. It still hasn't hit me.

Leaving Kankakee at 8 a.m., I arrive in Champaign by noon, having gone 80 miles in about four hours with one stop, which I work out to be about 22 mph for the day, almost double my pace from earlier days. I head to the quad at the university, lay the bike down, watch the students, and take a nap.

Waking up, I look at the trees and the direction they sway and realize I've had a 15-20 mph wind directly behind me all morning, which led to my increased speed. That won't happen often. Make the most of it.

I bike over to Boud's and feel the crosswind blasting me from the north. I'm still early. He's napping when I arrive, and I startle him. "Who the fuck are you?" he asks, jumping up from the couch in fear.

"Boud, man, it's me. Dave."

"Oh." He starts laughing. "I didn't recognize you."

As part of my trip, I'd cut my hair down as short as it would go and let my beard grow. He has never seen me with hair this short or the beginning facial growth.

The next day is on to Springfield and meeting up with college friends Phil Morettini and Jay Shattuck and his wife Mary.

Both are UofI buddies. Phil was on my dorm floor for two years, and we've stayed in close touch, playing basketball together, always up for a sports discussion. Jay roomed with me junior year at UofI, a warm, funny, and engaging man who had since gotten married to his high school sweetheart Mary and is beginning to carve a niche in Springfield, following his heart to become engaged in the political scene.

The wind is back in my face. It's unpleasant. Far too easy to get used to having it at my back. But I have to plug on.

After an easy day, you grow complacent. You think you'll get another easy day. That's not the case.

It's another 85-mile day, and as I close in on Springfield, I've had it emotionally, physically, and psychologically. I stop at a pay phone and call Jay, and he comes to pick me up. That's enough wind for a day.

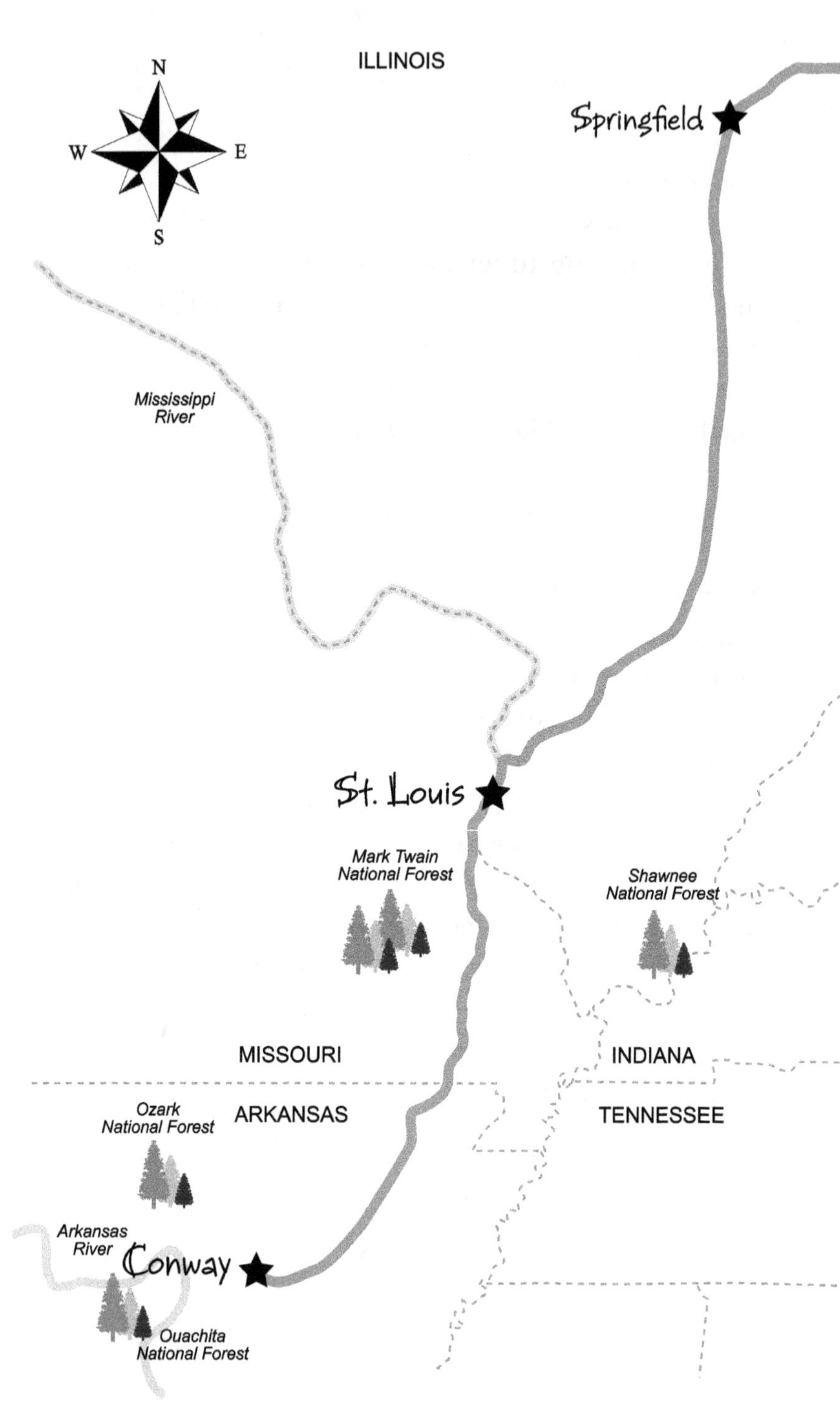
ILLINOIS
N
W
E
S
Springfield
Mississippi River
St. Louis
Mark Twain National Forest
Shawnee National Forest
MISSOURI
INDIANA
ARKANSAS
TENNESSEE
Ozark National Forest
Arkansas River
Conway
Ouachita National Forest

Chapter 3
Leaving the Comfort Zone

Heading south from St. Louis, I leave the comfort zone. For the first week or so I've been able to crash on a couch or bed at friends' houses. It's time to hit the road, pitch a tent, and find someplace safe each night. That produces anxiety.

Before leaving on the trip, multiple friends were concerned about my safety. Getting hit by a car or truck is certainly a possibility. Getting attacked by a stupid human at night could be another. Maybe a marauding bear or wild boar would annihilate my tent while I slept. I had my own fears and pushed them away. You couldn't even start the journey otherwise. Survival requires conquering fear. You must leave your comfort zone.

I get onto Missouri Highway 67, a two-laner undergoing construction to become four lanes. To the west, dirt has been moved and graded. You can see the two new lanes taking shape.

As the sun eases down, my anxiety increases. Where to camp? There are no state parks along the route, nor city parks. It's trees and occasional rolling farmland. Finally I decide to stop, walk my bike as far over as the two dirt tracks to the west, and set up my tent. I've been riding for eight hours. This area seems to provide a bit of protection, far enough off the road to prevent any marauding motorists. I want to be hidden and away from the noise as much as possible, and this seems the best option as the sun goes down. I looked for miles and miles, and this spot appears to be the best choice. I can burrow a bit into the woods and get away from the traffic to keep myself safe.

Cars roar by occasionally, preventing sleep. My tension being alone and sleeping by the side of the road also keeps me awake. Suddenly a car stops and a door slams. SHIT! I clamber for the tent zipper as a spotlight hits me. WTF?

It turns out to be a local police officer. I wasn't as hidden as I thought. A farmer called the police to report me camping. The officer appears as afraid of me as I am of him. He's a young man, probably my age (26), slightly overweight with a short blond buzz. He asks for ID and runs my driver's license. He comes back and asks a few questions. Where you from? How long you been riding? Where you headed?

He's probably looking at my super short hair and beard thinking I'm a punk rocker.

The conversation warms. We start sharing stories. He probably doesn't have much to do in a sparsely populated area like this and enjoys talking as much as I enjoy connecting with him. After fifteen or twenty minutes, he has to get back to his rounds, and I'm sorry to see him go. Once he leaves, I think we should have gone to the local eatery and grabbed a cup of coffee. To this day, I wonder if he remembers that meeting.

The following day is my first bath while on the road and another challenge figuring out where to safely sleep. You crave human contact when you are on a bicycle all day. There's a natural desire to have other people around at the end of the day.

Midday, I find a quiet stream by the side of the road and peel off my shirt, riding shorts, and underwear. I'm not using socks. There's a bar of ivory soap in the saddlebags for washing myself and my clothes. I change into my extra shorts, wet the dirty shirt and shorts, scrub, rinse, and set them on the bike to sit in the sun while I rest for an hour. They smell clean. The air is fresh. Birds sing. Spring permeates the air.

Later in the day, I'm again faced with where to sleep. There have been no towns, only occasional houses by the side of the road, and towards dusk, I stop to get some water at a house where kids are playing out front. I strike up a friendly conversation with the parents, who suggest I sleep in their backyard. I readily agree and pitch my tent. This type of kindness occurs repeatedly over the course of the tour.

***

The terrain grows hillier and more wooded with each passing day, though the riding is still relatively easy. Thunderstorms are in the air. You can smell them. The ability to predict the weather (and time) develops quickly. You feel the wind currents so you know which direction a system is coming from. You notice the change in moisture, signaling humidity and rain.

The sun wakes you up in the morning, giving you an initial time gauge. As it ascends during the day, you watch it trek across the sky and accustom yourself to where it is at all times. Very quickly I'm able to tell time in my head accurately within fifteen to twenty minutes.

Sensing impending storms, I seek cover for the evening. Again, no quick options emerge. I settle on a site under an overpass. BIG MISTAKE!

Almost as soon as I'm zipped in, the noises start. Something starts slapping the edge and top of the tent. My first thought is that it's local teenagers harassing me, but no way I wouldn't hear more noise if humans were traipsing about.

Is it a bear? Maybe a raccoon? A wild pig? Those thoughts, too, are quickly dismissed.

My body is rigid with fear, trying to figure out what the heck is going on. There are fluttering sounds, along with the slapping of the tent. It comes and goes.

Finally, I need to take leak, so I unzip the tent quickly and let out a loud scream, flailing my arms to ward off any intruders. I hear some scuttling but don't see anything out of the ordinary. Relieving myself, I look around and up. Sure enough, I see a bunch of pigeons. They've been dive-bombing me, those bastards! Amazing how your fear takes over.

Relaxed and with an empty bladder, I return to the tent and settle in for a comfortable evening. I look out at the brilliant night sky and see a light flash and dart. WHOA, a shooting star. Then there's another one. What the heck? Then I see a light go on and off in the distance. I take a big gulp. Is there a UFO out there? Did some satellites just fall from the sky?

Having defeated the pigeon fear, I'm faced with another

one, but now I'm fortified and ready to use logic. I concentrate on the light. Hmmm, it's not up in the sky; it's just hovering above the weeds. AH, it's fireflies.

If you're ever out camping alone and think you're seeing UFOs off in the distance, check your eyes first to see if it's fireflies. You'll sleep better.

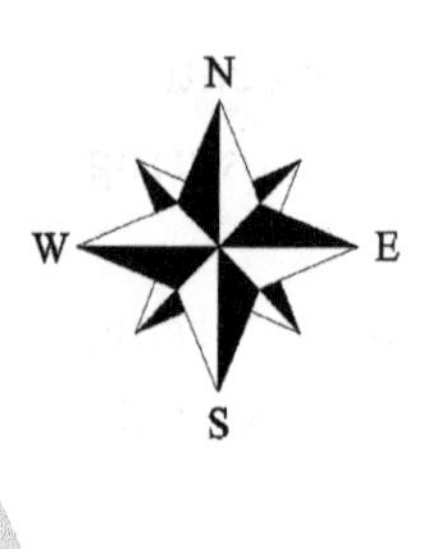

Ozark
National Forest

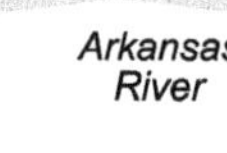

Nimrod

Toad Suck

Chapter 4
Snakes and Armadillos

When you thread the border into a new state on a bicycle, your mind imagines a significant demarcation, some geographical transformation at the border signaling you've entered new territory. There's not. The Ozarks spread through southern Missouri and northern Arkansas, the hills growing steeper, the trees denser. I switch maps to Arkansas after crossing the state line.

Thunderstorms threaten again. When you're hit by one, you want to avoid future encounters. I'm hoping for a small-town hotel on the road ahead.

The sun has baked me to a crisp brown. I'm lost in thought as a blue Mustang pulls up next to me with three teenage males inside, and one yells out the window, "Get off the road, nigger!" They peel off, laughing, exhaust smoke trailing. Incensed, I pop up the gears and race after them.

Thoughts of yanking them from the car and smashing their teeth in rage goes through my mind. Even as I pedal as fast as humanly possible, their car recedes in the distance. After 3-4 miles of explosive riding, I'm soaked and exhausted and dial back my anger and pedaling.

There is no blue Mustang in town, but there is a run-down

motel for $8.99 a night. I pay, walk my bike in, and examine the dump – no shower, paint peeling, soap that barely creates suds. But it's a roof over my head and safety from the approaching storm.

The water is hot in the tub, and I soak for a long time as the grime dissolves from my body. A black ring of dirt stains the tub afterwards. Rumbling comes closer, but I'm asleep before it hits. In the morning, the air is clean and the humidity is down.

***

The names of towns stand out. I pass through Nimrod, Arkansas, and play around with it in my head. "You Nimrod. Quit being a Nimrod." Makes you wonder how the town got named.

I pass through Toad Suck and Toad Suck Lock and Dam, spending hours afterwards playing around with the name, weaving imaginary short stories around it.

There are few towns with more than 20,000 souls in Arkansas, and I pass through only one on the journey – Conway. The roads are sparsely populated. Many homes have two or three trucks up on blocks for spare parts to keep another truck in running order.

Chickens and pigs are not uncommon on plots surrounding the homes. Many have large vegetable gardens, laundry hanging on the line, and large stacks of wood for heating and cooking. People appear more self-sufficient as you get further away from civilization.

Arkansas

Late one afternoon, I pull up to a country store. The owner, portly and balding, swings in his rocking chair. He is warm and inviting. We chat for a bit until a young man stops his church van in front of the store and gets out. The owner hails him, "Whattaya believe, son?"

"I believe in Jesus Christ as my Savior," he replies.

The young man is scrubbed clean, short hair, fresh clothes, and a wide smile. He's making the rounds for his church, spreading the gospel, handing out the pamphlets. This is the Bible Belt. You find out that people wear their religion on their sleeves more in the South, verbalizing their faith in Christ. As a northerner, this is new for me – a learning experience.

The owner inclines his head slightly, giving his assent for the young man to put out a stack of his literature in the store. The young man engages the store owner further, letting him know where the church is, when services are, and encourages his attendance before he hops into his van and off to the next small-town store. Spreading the word.

As he drives off, we resume our conversation, talking about where I'm from, where I'm headed. He's lived in the area his entire life. When you first meet him, you think he's a bit off, as he wears Coke-bottle glasses and is slightly cross-eyed. You'd be misjudging him though if you stereotyped that as not being up with things.

The guy is sharp as a steak knife in a high-end restaurant. He rocks in his chair, asking insightful questions, clearly interested in my journey. He offers observations on the country, the direction it's taking, and how things can be improved. It's a pleasant conversation, one that takes several different directions, and he offers consistently up-to-date viewpoints on what is going on. He's a reminder to me to get to know people. Don't assume, based on an initial perspective, that you know someone. There's always more there. There's always a story to tell.

He invites me to dinner at his house, a few miles back the route I've just come. I agree and push off. He closes the store and plans to join me in a few minutes.

Pedaling back to his house, there are two boys shooting hoops in the front yard, yelling, "It's Super Seed. He's got the ball. Super Seed shoots. He scores! Super Seed is dominating."

Who the heck is Super Seed? I play a lot of pickup basketball and am a bit of a student of the game, but I have no idea who these two kids are yelling about.

I ask the owner when he arrives. "That's Super Sid Moncrief

of the Milwaukee Bucks. He played here for the University of Arkansas."

Now I get it. He was one of the big three that put Arkansas men's basketball on the map, along with the Machine Gunner Marvin Delph (so known for his rapid fire, machine-gunning shot) and defensive specialist Ron Brewer. Local slang and a southern drawl threw me off. Super Seed will stay with me the rest of the trip, a story that speaks to local culture and the universal nature of basketball as something that brings us all together.

We eat heavy food, and I sleep like a rock. Carbed up, I wake with energy and hit the road early.

***

Throughout Arkansas, I notice dead animals on the highways, particularly turtles, armadillos, and snakes. It's a sad statement about gasoline-powered vehicles. They hurtle along with such speed that these creatures often have no chance to cross the road, getting splattered and crushed with regularity.

I try to count how many I see through the Ozarks and northern Arkansas, but the number is too great. Instead, I estimate how frequently I see a dead animal on the road. After several days of personal tracking, it turns out to be approximately one dead creature per mile. Though I'm not a big fan of snakes and don't have much knowledge of armadillos, the carnage bothers me when I think of our modern vehicles destroying precious wildlife.

On the bicycle, you are immersed in nature, tied to the local habitat, and able to see long stretches in front of you when a reptile or mammal is edging across the pavement. Multiple times I stop to help a turtle across. Why they cross the road is beyond me, but speaking with locals, it sounds like it has something to do with the time of year, mating season, laying eggs and getting back to their water habitat. But that doesn't explain why they were on the other side of the road to begin with. It's perplexing. A mystery for the trip.

***

Roads up the hills of the Ozarks tend to be steep. Rather than snaking side to side to decrease the incline, the engineers decided to head straight to the top. This makes for tough riding. I'm typically down in the lowest gear, pedaling standing up and out of breath by the time I reach the top of each new hill.

Looking down makes me think of roller coasters. I see how I can rocket down. After days of getting used to the speed of the descent, I become more and more daredevilish and finally decide to let it all out. Almost a BIG MISTAKE!

To gain speed like a bike racer, I drop my head down low on the handlebars and contract my body. This streamlines my speed to cut through the wind. A car passes me going the speed limit, around 55 mph. I coast to a stop, then push off to see how fast I can get down the hill.

It's exhilarating to feel the wind whip through my ears. I'm dialed into the surface of the road, hands locked to hold the bike steady. The slightest bump can set me off course.

I close in on the car, so I'm close to 55 mph when I hit a very small rock. The front wheel wobbles and veers off. I struggle with the frame, fighting the fall. Quickly I right my cycle, hit the brakes, and slow my speed. An adrenaline rush. Not one I wish to emulate in the miles ahead. One more lesson: I need to apply the brakes coming down big hills and mountains or I might not finish the journey.

The Ozarks

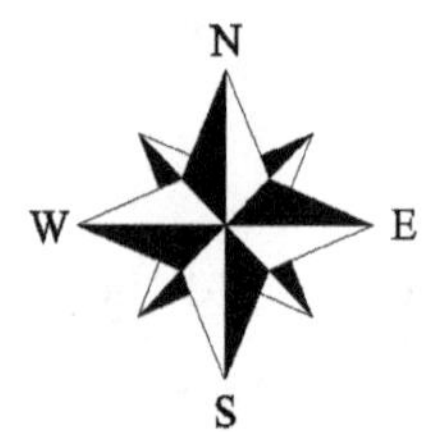

Fort Smith

Arkansas River

Plainview

Ouachita National Forest

OKLAHOMA

ARKANSAS

Broken Bow

Nashville

Chapter 5
Chased

One of the scary issues about bicycling across the country is the uncertainty. You don't know the upcoming terrain. You don't know what the weather holds. You don't know who or what you'll encounter while riding or setting up your camp at the end of the day.

So far, I've been lucky. Everyone I've met has been wonderful, kind, and helpful. That can't hold, and it doesn't.

After another long day (I'm averaging 60-100 miles per day at this point in the trip), I again pedal into a small town with no place to stay. There's no city park and no campgrounds anywhere nearby.

I could use a shower and a roof overhead for protection against more impending spring storms, so I seek out the local Salvation Army. They're supposed to be accepting.

It's clear when I arrive that I'm breaking into a clique. The guy who runs the building, Brad, has several local buddies hanging out with him, and I'm intruding. He doesn't want me there as he shoots me dirty looks and talks down to me. I don't know what I've walked into, but I don't want to look for another place, so I keep up the dialogue.

His grumpiness recedes ever so slightly after we talk more,

but he's still frowning, yacking with his buddies and doing his best to ignore me in hopes that I'll go away. After a bit, we sit down for dinner, say our prayers, and dig in. It's typical dorm-type, industrial-strength chow, but it hits the spot. The two other guys staying in the shelter for the night start asking me questions. Slowly we bond. They see I'm not a bad guy.

When you bike long distances, you become the permanent stranger, hat in hand, the vagabond that those you encounter have no way of knowing whether to trust, help, or attack. Because you're frequently in positions where people could take advantage of you, it's important to show you aren't a threat. The more real threat comes from those whose actions are directed at a bicyclist. There's nothing to stop something bad from happening to me. I'm alone. I have no witnesses defending me. I must rely on wits and goodwill. The good ol' boy network is alive and well at this Salvation Army.

I have my book to read. Brad takes my bike and stores it out back. It's lights out early.

Morning comes, and Brad seems more approachable. He greets me with a smile to start the morning. He's firing up grits and eggs on the griddle. It's filling. All three men pepper me with questions, wanting to know what Milwaukee is like, why I decided on the journey, where the physically most difficult days were.

The conversation transforms Brad. He opens up, asks questions. Whether he just had a good night's sleep or the grits and coffee hit him right, he's a new man this morning. It does appear that he's come to some form of consideration overnight to accept me into the fold. How will he look back on this encounter? I hope it is with openness.

Brad heads out and brings my bike back, shaking my hand, smiling, wishing me well. Another brief positive connection created. It's a good feeling as I pedal off.

***

I haven't met many other bicyclists out touring. That surprises me a bit. It might be that I've headed south and there aren't as many riders in this part of the country. Or it might be that I've taken a route in the middle of nowhere, through the Arkansas Ozarks.

That's about to change in an unexpected way. As I'm heading through another small town, a young man charges out in the road, waving his arms at me to stop. I pull over. He asks where I'm headed, and I respond, "Down to Dallas to see my brother and sister-in-law, then up to Kansas, out to Colorado, over to Washington state, then into British Columbia, and back through the southern section of Canada to Minnesota and Wisconsin." He's wide-eyed. He wants to know if we can grab dinner so he can quiz me on the trip. I readily agree.

When he gets off work, I meet him and another buddy, and we get food and head to his place for a few beers with the chow. He wants to do exactly what I'm doing. Tony recently graduated from high school and is working at the local hardware store. He's tall and rangy with long blond hair. He's enthusiastic about the trip and wants to join me but doesn't have the gear at this point.

My initial impression is that this is a great guy open to the world and its possibilities. He's been nowhere in his life. He's lived in a small town and never traveled beyond a state or two around his home. But he wants to. He wants to explore. A bicycle for him is a natural way to do this, meeting others, seeing the United States, expanding his horizons. I sense his need for this, to do more with his life, maybe answer some questions we all have during those teenage and early adult years. "What else is out there?"

My advice to him: "If you want to do it, go for it. You need a bike, tent, sleeping bag, some minimal clothes, and money for the length of your trip." I repeatedly encourage him to do it if

Arkansas

he's passionate about exploring the country. We finish eating, and I head off as there is still enough daylight left to get a few more miles down the road. It's not the last I'll hear of Tony.

***

Finding a place to sleep is a daily challenge. As I reach the western edge of Arkansas, I stop in a local supermarket and strike up a conversation with a young assistant manager in the dairy section. He's intrigued with my trip and offers his church's bus as an overnight place to sleep. More big thunderstorms loom for the area, and I accept the offer.

I wait for him to get off his shift, toss my bike in the back of his small white Ford Ranger pickup, and we're off to Oklahoma. It's a huge historical lesson as Will goes on and on and on about the paper mill we pass and the logging operation up the road. He tells me about the closed businesses, the challenge of finding a halfway decent job in the area, and his church's preacher.

"Father Jeb likes to preach."

"How long is his normal sermon?"

"Aww, he'll be talkin' for two or two-and-a-half hours."

My jaw drops. "Uh, you mean he'll still be preaching when we get there?"

"Yeah, he's only about half hour in right now. When we get there, he'll be about half done, so we'll be able to hear him for about another hour or so."

I've never heard of a sermon that long. It's a Pentecostal church, Will explains. All that means to me is they speak in tongues and handle snakes. In other words, I know nothing about Pentecostal services. I'm looking forward to the experience though.

The preacher is in full swing as we walk down the aisle and slide in next to Will's wife and two young children. The "AMENS" are flying. The preacher is ranting about wicked Oklahoma politicians taking $100 and $200 bribes and how they'll rot in hell. Spit is flying from his mouth. His face looks like a ripe tomato. I swivel around and watch as I hear from various parts of the congregation, "That's right, Jesus. Shame on them. PRAISE THE LORD. Preach it brother!"

The preacher's cadence picks up as the wailing and support from the congregation increases. He plays his audience like a fine fiddle. Will's kids are playing in the pew, punching each other and laughing, as Will and his wife nod and chant with the others.

Will is correct, and the preaching lasts a good while longer. When Father Jeb is exhausted, I am brought out for display like a newly minted Android. "I met this here young guy back at the supermarket and thought I'd bring him along to the service. He seemed like a nice man, and I told him he could sleep in our church bus for the night."

Everyone steps up to the newcomer, eyes wide, shaking my hand. "Glad to have you. Thank you for attending. Pleasure to meet you. God bless." It's a bit intense, but I hold my own. A prayer session follows, and attendees are encouraged to find their comfortable place to pray. I kneel and give thanks for the kindness given to me on the trip, for the help so many have provided, and for my personal safety.

As I'm silently sending my prayers, I hear wailing and crying. I open one eye. Will is rocking on his knees and very loudly chanting, "I want to thank you Jesus for everything you've done for me." Then he totally breaks down in tears. I'm flummoxed about what to do.

I open my other eye to look around. People have scurried off to different corners of the church, almost like bugs, and are leaning, rocking, wailing, crying, screaming, and chanting their message to Christ. I'm fascinated. Will's kids continue punching each other playfully, hopping up and down, and climbing on the pews like kids everywhere.

When the prayer session ends, I'm surrounded by well-wishers as we walk to the front of the church to get some food and locate the bus. In the back, there is a man in convulsions, legs and arms flailing. This concerns me. Two people appear to be subduing him. "What's going on?" I ask.

"Oh, he's getting the Holy Spirit," Will explains.

"What do you mean?"

"They're laying hands on him to bring the Holy Spirit into him and heal him."

After some homemade peanut brittle, I'm escorted out to the yellow school bus. It smells like every yellow school bus I've ever ridden in. I leave my bike up front, unpack my sleeping bag, and thank Will for his kindness. It promises to be another booming night.

Sure enough, massive storms rock the bus, and I say some more prayers of thanks for Will, these kind people, and the yellow school bus that protects me for another day.

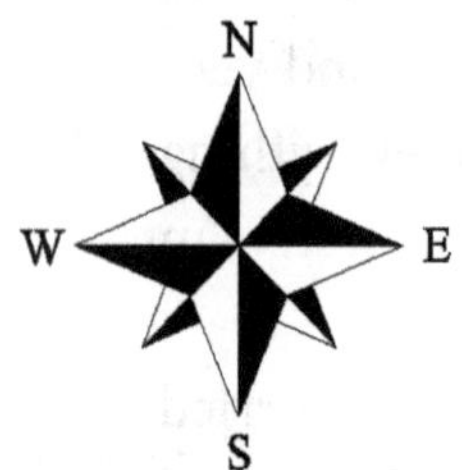

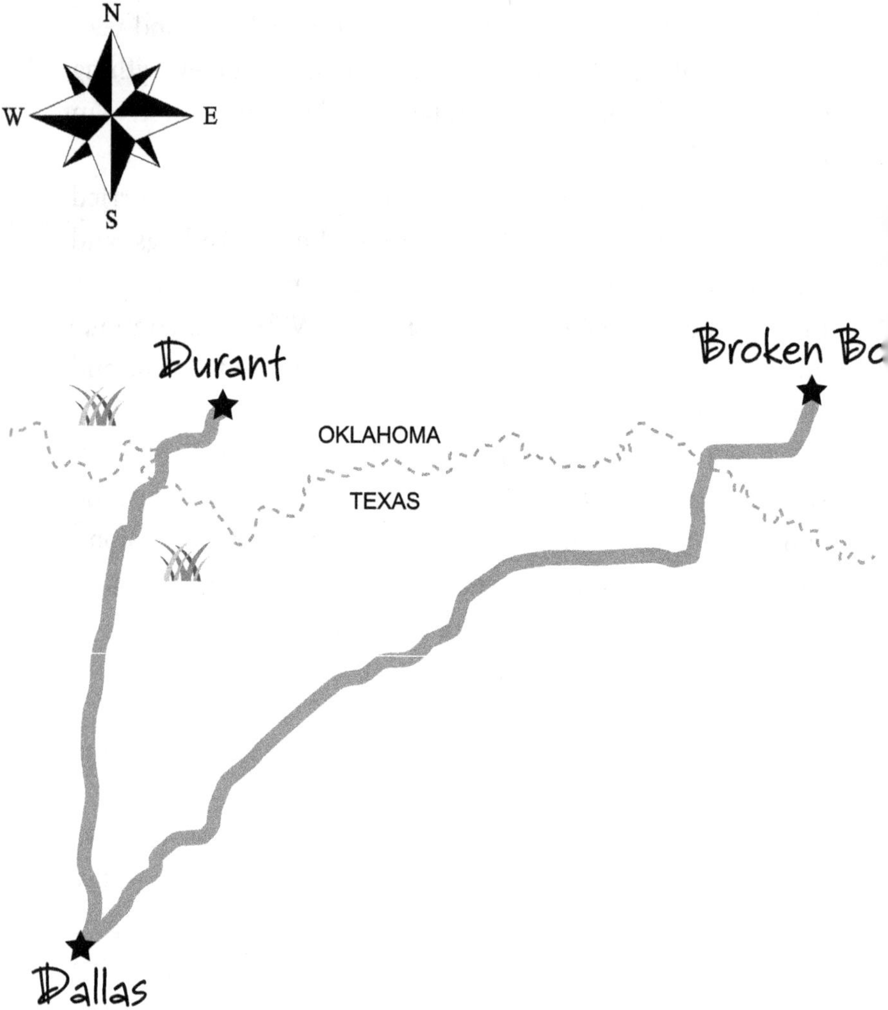
N
W
E
S
Durant
Broken Bo
OKLAHOMA
TEXAS
Dallas

Chapter 6
Re-entering Civilization

Leaving southern Oklahoma and closing in on the Dallas-Ft. Worth (DFW) metro area, the contrast from rural, open spaces to crowded roads with seemingly endless cars racing by stands clearly out. Density increases the pace of traffic. Rudeness of drivers increases as they no longer take time to pull to the left when passing. Part of that is logistical – there are so many cars, so there is no room. They zoom by me closely. I clench the handlebars tightly.

One safety measure you develop is a sixth sense of where cars are. Your smell, sight, and hearing are all enhanced when on a bicycle between six and ten hours a day. You pay attention. You listen intently. Hearing is your most important safety barometer, tuning your ears to cars coming up behind you. You feel their presence, know exactly what their distance is behind you based on their sound. If they're coming too close, you edge as far to the right as possible and look directly over your shoulder to see their specific location. You become good at this very quickly. Like any skill – use it a lot, and you become an expert.

Heading into Dallas to my brother Peter and his wife Pat's house, I'm ready for a HUGE meal. I called the night before,

My brother Peter and his wife Pat

and Pat asked what I'd like. Eating few carbs for more than a week leaves me savoring. I ask for spaghetti.

Not only does Pat prepare a spaghetti feast which I inhale to the tune of three full portions, but some new product has just come out called "Cookies 'n Cream" ice cream. Sounds good to me. Polishing off the salad, spaghetti, and rolls isn't enough to sate me, so just for good measure, I have two bowls of this delicious, newly invented ice cream.

It's a bad idea. You forget your stomach contracts when eating mostly protein, fruits, and granola for days on end while biking 90 miles a day burning off calories. The gut is not ready.

After dinner, I crawl on their floor and groan. It reminds me of Thanksgiving when you are a kid, you eat way too much, and your stomach cannot expand to digest it. My sides split. I moan away, rolling on my gut to try and get comfortable.

It's like knives are being jammed into various parts of my abdomen. Though the pain seems to go on forever, I'm sure it's not more than an hour or two.

Dallas is good for a recharge, catching up with Peter and Pat, and taking in a Charlie Daniels concert. It's the second time I've seen him live, and he seems way more kickass than the first time I heard him. He wails on the fiddle in "The Devil Went Down to Georgia." Maybe it has to do with the trip.

There's something odd about being back in civilization. It's comforting on one hand. Staying with Peter and Pat gives me the roof and bed, so that's taken care of. I don't have to be on edge. I sleep better and longer.

On the other hand, when staying inside, I lose the rhythm of the outdoors. The sun and birds don't wake me like they have the past two weeks. It's a bit disconcerting. Because I grow accustomed to nature when I'm outside all day, being back inside is not the norm. That's one of the biggest adjustments in the days I spend in Dallas – no longer being connected to the weather, land, and changing nature of each day.

My other main observation upon reentering civilization has three parts: traffic, crowding, and growth. DFW is a huge metro area and is growing at an astronomical pace. People seem to be everywhere. This is a tough adjustment. On the bike, you have an aloneness almost all day, every day. Riding with Pete and Pat in the car or being with them at the concert, it seems like people are everywhere.

The country in the United States is wide open. In DFW, you see how we are redefining the places we live – smaller towns getting smaller and bigger cities getting bigger. The city offers excitement, entertainment, and endless food choices. Out on the road, it's bananas, apples, granola, kippers, sardines, and peanut butter, and no conversation.

Traffic, crowding, and growth tie together. Because DFW has become a place to be, people have moved here from all over the U.S. There's a mix of cultures, attitudes, and opinions. Biking across rural parts of the country and spending a lot of time in tiny towns, you get a much stronger sense of place and spirit of the community.

Neither is right or wrong, but both reflect what is going on in the country, trends that accelerate. On a bicycle, you see and feel these things directly. They're tangible.

In the metro area, I feel less comfortable. Maybe it's because I've become accustomed to the bike and the trip. Despite my enjoyment with Peter and Pat, I want to get back to the open spaces and constant moving, less constrained and hemmed in by cars and trucks.

***

Leaving DFW is bittersweet – tough to leave the family and good food and safe lodgings, but good to stretch the legs again and be moving. The road beckons.

It's still May, still thunderstorm season. The first night out from DFW, I'm not prepared for what happens.

I hit the Texas-Oklahoma border with no incident. The terrain is slightly hilly, a few scrub trees here and there, then more deciduous into Oklahoma. I find a state park where I'm allowed to stay for free.

Titanic oak trees tower throughout the camping area. I find a soft site covered in pine needles, place my bike against a tree, and set up tent. My sardines and banana hit the spot. I write in my journal. The light leaves the sky quickly because of the dense canopy of leaves. The booming starts in the distance.

It doesn't take long before the campgrounds are rammed by rain torrents, lightning blasts peppering the area. I huddle in the tent. Though dry, my body remains tense as God keeps rolling the bowling ball and striking the pins overhead. The crashes and flashes keep me awake for hours. Not until the storm pushes off to the north and east is my body able to ease up and finally find sleep.

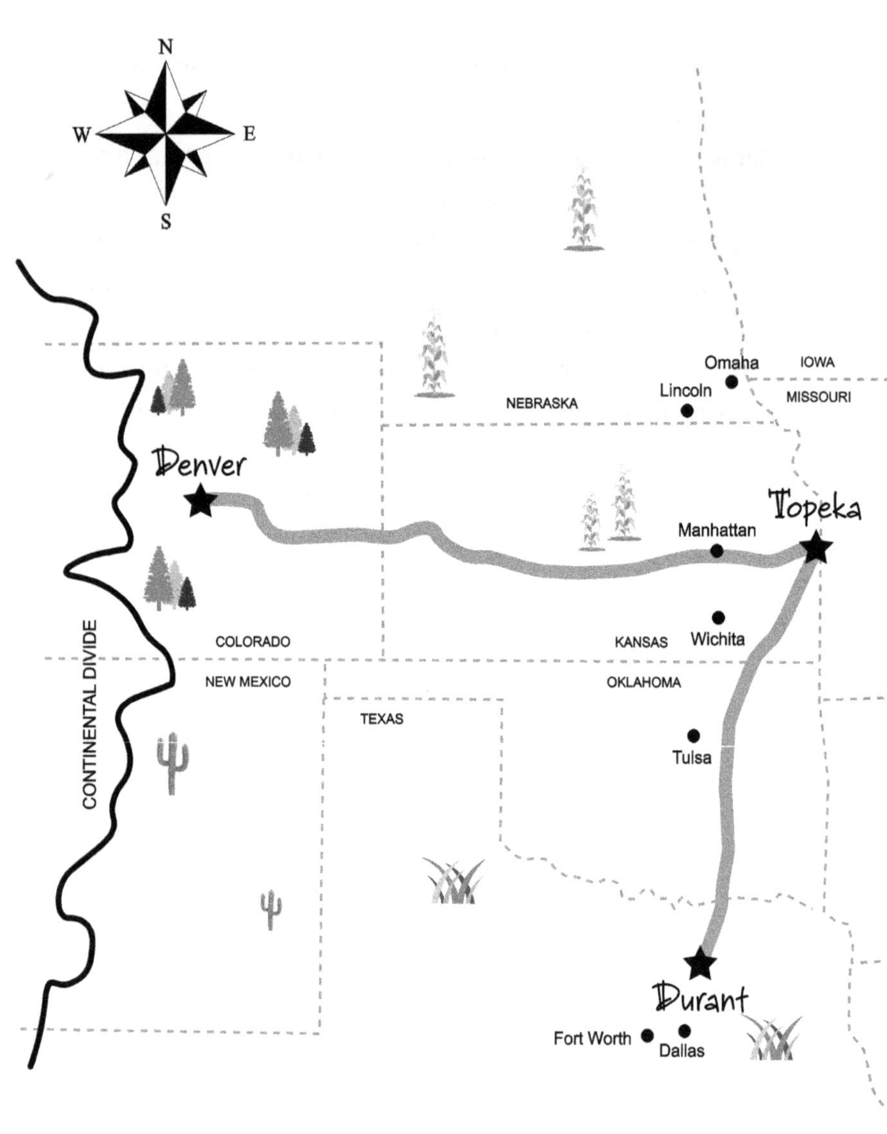

N
W
E
S
CONTINENTAL DIVIDE
Denver
COLORADO
NEW MEXICO
TEXAS
NEBRASKA
Omaha
Lincoln
IOWA
MISSOURI
Topeka
Manhattan
KANSAS
Wichita
OKLAHOMA
Tulsa
Durant
Fort Worth
Dallas

Chapter 7
The Heartland

The Oklahoma and Kansas countryside is open, the roads bad. Arkansas, Oklahoma, and Kansas have some of the worst roads I've ridden on – crumbling, bad surfaces, in need of repair. You notice these things more on a bicycle.

Heading north to Kansas, people get sparser and cows more populous. I take to mooing on a regular basis to get their attention and see if they respond. It's a weird thing about the trip: Going solo pushes you into strange places. You think you can communicate with animals.

I practice daily projecting the moo into the herds of cattle. Typically, there are several responses. Oddly, the movement of the bicycle startles them, and they trot off into the distance before stopping to observe me. They are used to cars and trucks, and the speed and noise don't affect their behavior at all. But for some reason, a bike quietly riding by seems to puzzle them. I'm guessing because it's an atypical sound and movement. They don't see a lot of people like me on a bicycle, slowly puttering by, so they have no frame of reference – if cows have a frame of reference. This makes me think of Gary Larson cartoons when the cows act stupid if humans are around, then pop up onto two legs and start having conversations as soon as we're out of the picture.

The second response is a quizzical look. I moo. They turn their heads with a facial expression of, "Who you trying to kid?" I think to myself, "Made you look."

It becomes a game. I try different tones and projections, sometimes bellowing, sometimes softly sending a greeting. They roll their eyes, chew their cud, flick their tails, bend their heads, and grab some extra grass in their mouths.

The third response appears to be herd behavior. If one of the cattle spooks the rest, you can see how stampedes start. That must be where the phrase originated about "herd mentality" behavior or "acting like cattle." One does it and the rest follow without thinking, just like humans.

The last evening camping before cycling into Topeka is spent at a park just off Highway 75. There's a large lake near the highway where I pitch my tent. It's hot to start the morning, and I walk to the lake to jump in for a refresher before hitting the road. I bend down, look at the water, and see a snake swimming away from the edge. Uh, nope, not gonna take a swim this morning.

***

My mom and dad have been totally supportive of my trip, though Mom expressed reservations about my safety. They've always encouraged my siblings and me to pursue our dreams, spread our wings, explore the world. I'm anxious to see them.

Max, our family's current dog, is a porky, lovable golden retriever. He greets me with his usual tail wag and friendly face.

Maybe it's my skinniness from being on the road so long, but man, does he look heavy.

Topeka helps me pack on a few pounds from Mom's phenomenal cooking. I haven't seen her and Dad since Christmas, when our family annually gathers to catch up. They're in their mid-50s, healthy, active, playing tennis and golf. There's a strong reconnection as I spend time with them, thinking about some of the lessons they taught me and my two

Dad

Mom

At my parents' house

brothers about going after things in life. That message has been part of the fuel for this trip – taking on a major challenge to see if I can do it. It's not quite the halfway point, but I feel like I'm in a good space.

I catch up on sleep, laze around, read, do some writing. While there, I call Peter. He tells me that Tony, the young man from Arkansas, has showed up in Dallas, looking to catch up with me. "NO WAY! Are you serious?" I ask him.

"Absolutely. We gave him Mom and Dad's address in Topeka so he can keep following you. Hopefully he can catch up and you can ride together."

"That'd be awesome." After five days of recuperation, heavy food replenishment, and comfortable nights of sleep, it's time to push west.

At my parents' house with Max

***

The first night out of Topeka, I'm heading west towards Manhattan on Highway 24. It feels good to be back on the road, but pain is catching up. My knees are sore. My butt hurts. My hands are stiff. The repetitive motion of pedaling so many miles each day catches up with me.

To relieve the soreness, I find ways to ride differently. Taking pressure off the butt means riding standing up. I'll spend miles pedaling upright to get brief relief. As the hands stiffen up, I go to riding with no hands and relive memories of pedaling my bicycle to and from school in New Jersey with no hands on my 3-speed Stingray. No matter how much you vary the routine, you still cope with pain. It will not go away. You can only limit it for short periods of time. It's another life lesson in many ways: We all deal with different types of pain in our lives, and how we cope, adjust, and work through it says a lot about who we are. More pain is in the offing for the evening.

I find a good park to camp at the end of the first day out of Topeka. It's just outside Manhattan, filled with RVs and a few other tent campers surrounding a small pond. That day has been humid. I disembark and set up the tent near the pond. Ominously, mosquitoes start to attack the netting. It is like an army has decided to invade. They whine and flick against the screen. It is the thickest I've seen them since starting the trip, and I wonder why. Is it the water nearby and they have a breeding ground? Is it the time of year? Are there more mosquitoes in Kansas than Oklahoma, Arkansas, or Missouri?

You make a lot of observations when you're out in the middle of nowhere with only your wits to help you. A huge one involves the weather. You come to own it. You don't need to see a TV or read a newspaper with someone talking about what to expect. Instead, you live it every day. You feel moisture in the air. The shift in wind currents can be subtle, but it means a ton when you're on a bicycle. It may signal a storm is coming in, or crisp, cold Canadian air is going to start pouring down from the north. You understand how important it is for farmers to know when the rain will come, when to plant crops and cultivate. They must be attuned to the earth, the way I've become on the trip. It's something lost on most people in modern societies these days, a sad indictment as we lose connection to the earth that sustains us.

You also come to sense things more intimately the longer you spend time outside. Sounds carry great distances. You forget that when you hear car traffic all day. Instead, when I camp or stop to rest and let the silence envelop me, the slightest noise stands out. It could be a deer crunching in the underbrush. It might be the wind picking up ever so slightly. The hoot of an owl or the yelp of a coyote stands out so much more when your senses are adjusted to your surroundings. Tonight, it's the mosquitoes that start making noise.

The mosquitoes, dense air, and very slight trembling of the earth scare me – a monumental storm is on the way. The air is dead. The mosquitoes swarm. The earth starts to shake more and more. BOOMING begins WAY in the distance. It's coming closer. The mosquitoes are layered on the front screen of my tent, almost like they've been painted thickly there.

There is no way to brace for a storm like this. One moment all is still. The next, a heartland thunderstorm threatens to take me away. Lightning is everywhere. The wind is outrageous. My small tent can't hold the water out.

I decide to get out, yank the stakes out of the ground, and run under a shelter, getting soaked in seconds. I place the tent on top of the green picnic table under the shelter and quickly clamber back inside, shivering. Through the tent, I grip the edges of the table and hold on for dear life. The wind buffets me horizontally. It's crazy how powerful it is. Gusts hit me over and over and over. My arms cramp. More water seeps into the tent despite being under the roof. I pray for God to get me through the night.

As suddenly as the thunderstorm rips through, it stops. There's a trickle of lighter rain, then it's gone. In the morning, I climb out, thank God for giving me another day, and kiss the ground.

The previous evening, the campground was full, mostly with RVs and maybe five or six tents. This morning there are four RVs left. Everyone else pulled up stakes and went home. I survived.

I knock on the RV next to me, and a husband and wife come to the door and invite me in. "Why didn't you come over and get cover with us when the storm started?" they ask me.

Honestly, the idea never occurred to me. I felt like I had to gut it out myself. Looking back, I should have asked to come in for safety. I promise myself not to take those chances again.

Slowly making my way through the debris, it is like a war

zone in the camp. Tree limbs are downed everywhere. I must navigate everything from twigs to huge branches that the wind ripped and tossed aside.

Arriving in Manhattan, I break one of my vows: Don't read a newspaper or watch the television news for the entire trip. For the only time during the journey, I purchase a newspaper to read about the storm. It turns out that sustained winds of 88 mph hit the area. Funnel clouds appeared in several spots, but no tornadoes touched down. Again, I give thanks for surviving and ask, "What more do you have in store for me?"

***

My knees, butt, and hands continue to dog me. I've been on the road for over a month, and despite respites in Dallas and Topeka, the nonstop pedaling wears down the joints and muscles impacted by the repetitive motion.

Continuing up Highway 24, towns become sparser, smaller. Filling up on water, I strike up a conversation with Sam, a traveling salesman. He clearly likes to talk and has many opinions of the future of the United States and how we are about to crash. "Debt is the problem. Our government is in debt. Too many people are in debt. That's why I pay cash for everything," he proudly tells me.

He asks if I want a ride, and I readily agree – an opportunity to rest and get some views out in the hinterland. He regales me with stories as he sails his boat-like car across the parched Kansas outback. Not much to see other than brown grass and slightly rolling hills. You sneeze, and the towns are gone. He shares his view on how to survive the coming apocalypse – stay debt-free.

We say our goodbyes in a small western Kansas town that has a tiny park where I can crash for the evening. A few kids stop by to talk, but otherwise it's an uneventful evening.

The next day I ride to the Kansas-Colorado border. There's anticipation building about the Rocky Mountains and what it will be like to cycle up and down. One of my college roommates, Scott Norgaard, lives in Denver and will be my next rendezvous point.

It's cold the last evening before reaching Denver. The air is crisp with no clouds, so it feels like the warmth is slipping out of the earth. It's a good night to have a thick sleeping bag. I don't.

In the morning, I can see my breath. I also see a flat on my back tire. Fuck. I pull out one of the spare inner tubes and accidently stab it. I can tell I've poked a hole in it, so I patch that, along with the first one, and pull out my second spare inner tube to insert it on the wheel base. The rubber of the wheel is hard to stretch out, and as I pop it finally into place after a struggle with my numb hands, I fear I've once again punctured the inner tube. I pump it up. Yup. It immediately deflates. Fuck again.

One inner tube left. I try to be gentle. That does not appear to be in my makeup. The cold air hardened all the rubber. The last inner tube springs a leak. Time to hitchhike.

I walk my bike up to the road and stick out my thumb. I

have no hesitation hitching a ride. It's become clear that people trust me on the bike, and I've developed full trust in those who choose to stop. They're curious. They want to know what I'm doing, where I've been, where I'm headed. And I've got stories to share and questions to ask them. We need more of that trust today. Hitchhiking is one of those connections we used to have with others which has gone the way of black and white TV.

Quickly, a young guy in a pickup stops. We talk nonstop into Denver, and he drops me off at Scott's.

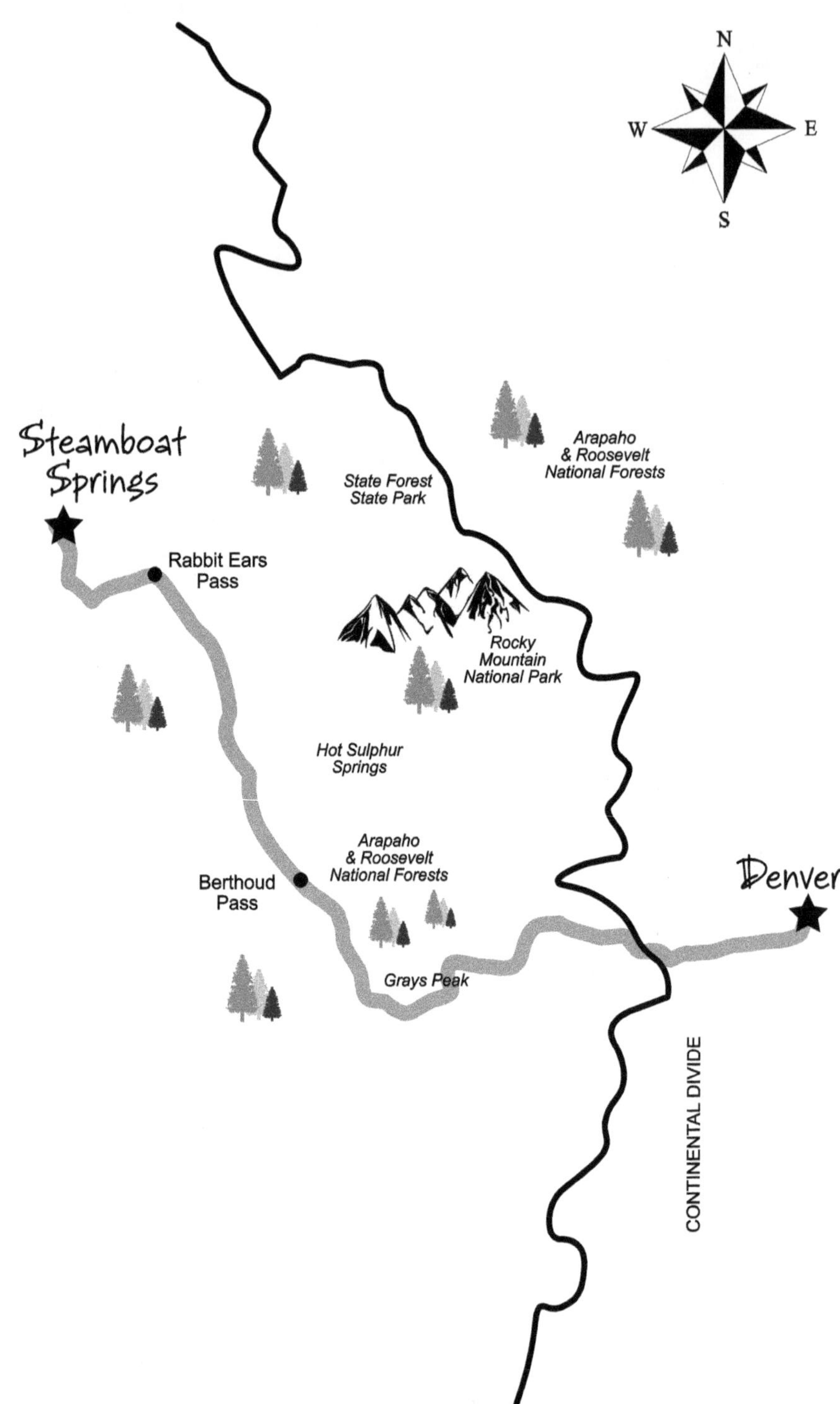
N
W
E
S
Steamboat Springs
State Forest State Park
Arapaho & Roosevelt National Forests
Rabbit Ears Pass
Rocky Mountain National Park
Hot Sulphur Springs
Arapaho & Roosevelt National Forests
Berthoud Pass
Denver
Grays Peak
CONTINENTAL DIVIDE

Chapter 8
The Rockies

My first impression getting dropped off at Scott's house is that he has a nice little bungalow. It makes me think of the west. Not a log cabin, but a "cabin-ish" feel. I'm hungry. Scott likes cheese. He pulls a hunk out of the fridge and starts breaking off chunks. We inhale them in monumental bites. My salivary glands go nuts, and my stomach experiences nirvana.

Denver is becoming a destination city. I can feel the vibrancy and funkiness as Scott drives me around and pulls up at a local restaurant. Lots of young people. Very outdoorsy. Bicyclists abound. This became noticeable biking through Kansas and into Colorado. Further east, drivers are more impatient. They honk at times. They don't give you much room on the roads.

Hitting western Kansas and cycling into Colorado, you sense, feel, and see a difference. More people ride. You're given a wider berth by drivers. You get head nods and waves. It's a good feeling. I've started to see other cross-country cyclists packed with large saddlebags.

That biking aura extends to the Denver area. People dress more casually in clothes designed for the outdoors. The menu reflects a healthier, back-to-the-earth selection of food. Any food that is not fresh fruit, granola, or some transportable light protein feels like an indulgence. I'm ravenous and eat like I'll never have food again.

We take in the German movie *Das Boot*, and being in a movie theater after so many weeks on the road is strange. Perhaps it is not having seen any media for so long, but I'm gripped by the tale like few movies I can remember.

The movie takes place in a submarine as the sailors get trapped. The claustrophobia of the cramped quarters kicks me in the gut. I feel my stomach knotted with the intensity of them trying to get the sub operable again, the potential to be stuck at the bottom of the ocean. Having been out in the open for so long on my bicycle, seeing a movie, and seeing something this intense, smashes all my senses. My hands tightly grip the arm rest. I feel my stomach muscles knot. I can't take my eyes off the screen.

Leaving the theater is what it must be like to be released

"Dress up" outfit

from prison. There's a deep exhale that you made it. That's how I feel as we stroll hipster Denver, light air, lots of foot traffic, people out for a stroll enjoying the evening. The movie stays with me long afterwards.

***

I call home to Topeka to speak with Mom and Dad. "David, this nice young man just stopped by. He told us he is trying to catch up with you. We gave him Scott's address. We hope that's okay," Mom tells me over the phone. It's Tony. Unbelievable. He's continuing to track me, and he's closing in. I hope he picks up the pace. It would be awesome to have someone to ride with. Loneliness is your constant companion.

I stay a few days with Scott, taking my bike into a local shop. Beyond the flat tire issues coming into Denver, I've counted up twenty-two flats so far on the trip, far too many. The repair guy has a solution, something I've never heard of – thorn-resistant inner tubes. They're incredibly thick. Plus, he pumps a sealant inside. If the inner tube does puncture (way more unlikely now), the sealant ebbs into the crack and helps keep air from flowing out. We'll see how it goes.

A couple of nights before I'm to leave Denver, we meet with Scott's sister Pat and brother-in-law Randy Fortin. Randy is intrigued with my quest, having considered a long bike trip before, but has never gone forward. Now he decides to join me on a spur of the moment. It's only for a few days, but it's good to have someone along.

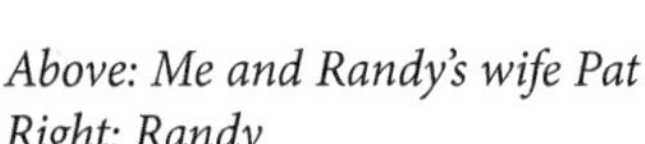

Above: Me and Randy's wife Pat
Right: Randy

We head out of Denver up the Rockies. It's a slow ride through Golden and up to Berthoud Pass. For the first time on the trip, I'm having real trouble with stamina. I can't figure it out.

To get to the top of Berthoud Pass, the road switches back over and over. This makes for a more gradual rise – a good thing. Still, I'm getting dizzy and having head rushes.

Randy and I stop to talk. He's feeling it too. It's the elevation, something I hadn't considered. We slow our pace and stop a couple more times as we keep chugging along. Looking down is scary. The edges of the road are steep, and if you get swiped or lose your balance, it's game over.

At the top, there is a ski slope. It is mid- to late-June. We're told the slope closed the previous week. Snow continues to cover the mountain, and the air chills at the top. It's fucking cold!

We stop to enjoy the wide-open vista and put on our warmest clothes. I don't have much. There's a sweatshirt, rain jacket, and some cheap gloves. I didn't plan on cold weather this close to July.

Covered as well as possible, we shove off and accelerate. Going down takes the same back and forth path, but Randy and I are light on the brakes, so we speed up and are crushing it. I condense my body, almost like trying to curl it into a ball, in an attempt to retain warmth. My hands go numb. I start chattering.

By the time we hit Winter Park, I'm having the full body shakes. We debark and stop at a local café to get some soup and warm up. It feels like walking into a quaint chalet from the 1950s – warm, cozy, welcoming. The soup helps immensely, but daylight is seeping away, and we need to get a campground just north of town.

We hit the grounds as it gets dark. Randy has a gargantuan sleeping bag designed for below-zero temperatures. Mine is good to 32 degrees Fahrenheit. We start a fire, eat some snacks, shoot the shit. He shares dreams of taking a trip across the U.S., a dream he'll realize many years later.

I'm still bone cold, unable to warm up. Randy is toasty in his sleeping bag and covers his head with his underwear. He sleeps smiling. It's a long time before I'm warm enough to crash.

We wake to frozen water bottles. It's hard to believe that

in late June it can still get below freezing. We restart the fire to warm up and quickly get moving on the road to get the blood flowing.

Today we hit another pass – Rabbit Ears. It's north of Winter Park. Fairly easy biking until we hit the climb. Then it's a steep, rapid ascent. We both struggle. We stop to rest. Then we start again. Unlike Berthoud, the road to this pass hasn't been constructed with as much forethought. We stop and walk a bit, talk it over, and decide to see if we can catch a ride. It doesn't take long. A pickup truck stops, and we toss our bikes in back.

That night, the weather seems the exact opposite of our first evening together. It's hot, and there's even a touch of humidity for the middle of the Rockies. Mosquitoes come out early, driving us into our tents to continue our discussions. You hear them whine and pop the side of the tent, like an infestation.

We say our goodbyes the next day as Randy heads west and south to catch up with Pat. I'm heading northwest to Utah and Idaho.

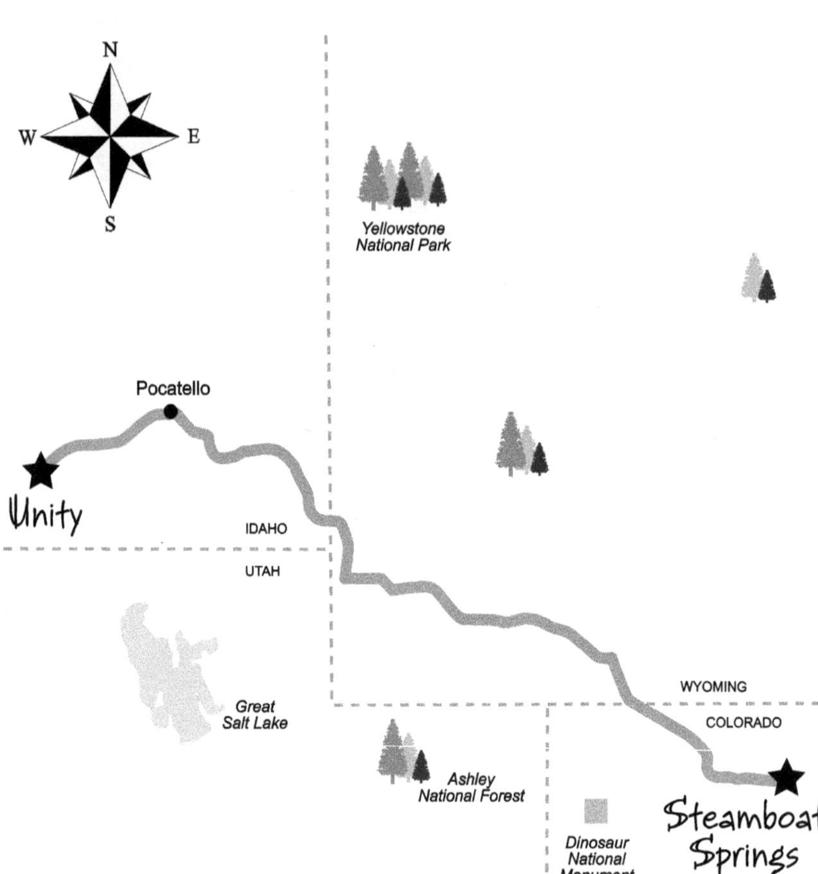
N
W
E
S
Yellowstone
National Park
Pocatello
Unity
IDAHO
UTAH
Great
Salt Lake
WYOMING
COLORADO
Ashley
National Forest
Dinosaur
National
Monument
Steamboat
Springs
Fishlake
National Forest

Chapter 9
Utah and Idaho

I get lonely quickly without Randy along. I'd already gotten used to having someone to bounce things off and keep from going crazy. Without him, it's back to living constantly in my head.

Despite the feel of being surrounded by the majestic Rockies, the nonstop pedaling grinds me down physically, mentally, and emotionally. My knees have been acting up. It feels like a sharp knife has been stuck into both butt cheeks any time I adjust on the bike seat. My hands are stiff, and the upper left side of my back throbs. Other than that, I feel great.

Emotionally, it's a different story. When you sign up for a trip like this, you don't realize how much alone time you'll have and how much you end up existing in your head. You take the terrain as it comes, but mentally and emotionally, you often fade into your past or project into the future. The present moves slowly.

I find myself reliving many moments of my life, wondering if I should have changed something or taken a different path. I look into the future and wonder how our country will change in the years ahead, whether we're putting too much stress on the environment, and what that will mean when the earth revolts.

It's easy to ride the emotional roller coaster. Up and down. Soaring highs yodeling and creating bizarre songs that rip from my lungs. Valley-like lows as I pound through another day with no one to share my thoughts with. I deeply realize how important human companionship is. We cannot survive without it. It gives each of us great meaning in our lives. Those connections made while biking often sustain me for days in my memories.

Long stretches of arid land with few trees stretch between the mountains. Towns seem newer out here. You don't get the sense of history in the communities in western Colorado like you do on the east coast of the U.S.

Crossing into Utah, there is something wrong with my rear wheel. I don't know what, but the wheel has begun to bend out of shape and rub on the brake pads. I don't have a clue what's going wrong, since my mechanical knowledge stops at "righty tighty, lefty loosey," but I know I need to get the issue checked, so I stop in the first town that has a bike shop.

Turns out I have broken spokes which need to be replaced. Ironically, they don't have any in stock, so the owner trues up the rim, straightening it as best he can so that I can make it to a bigger town and get the replacement spokes.

I meander around town for a bit, and because it seems clean and safe, decide to camp in a local park. It's wide open, used for soccer. Basketball courts are off to one side, and there's a large pavilion. I pitch the tent next to the pavilion, pull out my book, and read until it is dark.

Once you get used to taking care of yourself and not having

anyone around at night, you learn to trust your instincts and fall asleep quickly. Exhaustion takes over. But you also have to talk yourself through fears of weird sounds, ones you'd never hear if you were home in bed.

Tonight though, that's not the case. Getting to sleep is no problem. Waking up is.

I hear noises in the grass nearby, a hissing and clicking sound. Instantly, I'm alert. "What the hell?"

There's a watering noise, and it sounds like someone is standing next to my tent, taking a titanic piss on it. I curse to myself, "Why would someone do that?" The piss is over in seconds. Whew.

I hear another "cachink, cachink" sound, and then someone else is taking a heavy leak on the side of the tent. Dammit. I'm getting upset and can't figure out what the heck is going on. I'm awake and starting to pull myself together when the sound comes back around, and the watering of the tent hits again.

This pushes me to action, and I clamber out, ready to fight. The field is wide open. The sun is not yet up over the eastern edge of the Rockies. There's not a cloud in sight. It's a beautiful, high, dry morning. I scan the area. Nothing.

Then I see it: a sprinkler system. The "cachink" sound is the sprinkler shifting its arc around the field. I watch as it makes its wide circle and hits my tent again, soaking the edge briefly for the fourth time. Sigh. So much for conquering our fears.

***

After eating my morning munchies and refilling my water bottle, I find a guy who is staying in the area in his truck camper. He is a contractor employee, roaming the western part of the U.S., taking IT jobs when it suits him, working for months at a time then taking off and moving someplace else. A modern nomad.

He cooks me breakfast, and I decide to ride along with him for the day. He gives me a rundown on why he likes this part of the country, the influence of Mormons in the area, and places to camp in the coming weeks. It's good information.

A day after we separate, I end up at Dinosaur National Monument in Jensen, Utah. It's a first-time "tourist" day. The site is being excavated in live time, so you can see the bones and fossils slowly being outlined by the employees as they pick, dust, and wash the rock. You realize the vegetation necessary to keep dinosaurs alive was fully available millions of years ago in this area. Now it's rock and desert. Little water, few trees.

While there, I meet a group from Seattle, Washington. They came east for a camping, outdoor vacation and ask if I'd like to ride along with them, so I hitch a ride up the highway, making another new set of friends. Tom is the driver, and he gives me his contact information for me to stop and see them when I hit Seattle. Little does he know, I'll take him up on that offer.

***

Finding a campsite is a crapshoot. I continue to pick up a new map every time I cross a state line. There is no preconceived notion of what's next, so I keep following the highways I'm on and look for interesting places to visit as well as possible local, state, or federal parks where camping is allowed.

Pulling into Park City, Utah, north of Salt Lake City, the mountains seem steeper, the air cleaner, the people younger and more well-to-do. There's a strange, changing vibe here.

Old cabins are being knocked down and fresh condos are going up. Everyone seems to have bright-colored shirts and shorts on and to have come from money. The faces are freshly scrubbed. People smile. They act friendly. Mormons!

In talking with some locals though, you hear undercurrents. People who have lived for a long time in the community are being forced out due to costs. Those who work the ski lift and in the restaurants and resorts can no longer find affordable housing. They're moving to smaller towns down the road or packing four or five people into cabins or apartments that are meant to house one or two people just so they can make rent.

The land is gorgeous, but I sense that only the wealthy can afford to live here. I pedal north and west, find a nice wooded park, and for the first time on the trip, I build a campfire. I tend to live in my head all day, so contemplating my day while sitting around a campfire doesn't provide any new insights. With enthusiasm I accept a large Foster's Lager can from a man on the site next to me.

He invited me over to join him and his wife around their campfire. You get a quick buzz when you haven't had an adult beverage in a while. We tell stories and gaze at the stars, which seem close enough to grab. We laugh, listen to the pop of the dry wood, watching the sparks dazzle us as they burst up from the flames.

I feel a touch of sadness saying goodnight. I sleep well, feeling safe and warm.

***

The Rockies slowly start calming down, the peaks rounding off and turning into hills, then smaller hills. I've never been to Idaho. Pocatello is my next stop, and I encounter another first: true hobos. They seem like bums you would see in movies from the 1950s, living with the clothes on their backs, hitching trains, bumming meals, sometimes working when the spirit hits them, but for the most part living day-to-day and not caring about much else.

Meeting them provides an eye-opening experience. They've been all across the United States and regale me with stories about jumping on moving trains, not knowing where they'll end up, and hopping off to explore a new location when they feel the urge to stop traveling. You wonder what it would be like.

Almost all are white (one African-American guy) and from the west coast. I'm guessing they're between the ages of twenty-five and fifty, and for some reason didn't want the responsibilities of a working life, instead choosing the vagaries of the road. To a man, they seem to enjoy their status; it's almost like bragging rights that they get by on their wits. They sneer at people working full-time.

Their clothes are ratted, and they have that stale body odor you smell around people who haven't bathed or washed their clothes for a long period of time. Their faces are ruddy and sunburned, that outdoor look you see in people who are in the sun and wind for weeks on end. They have a camaraderie that you see in small tribal units. Like their own little society, you're only allowed in if you prove yourself, get specifically invited, or have been around long enough to achieve icon status. None of these guys are rookies.

Camping that evening, a slow train moves close to the grounds where I'm sleeping. I can hear the "click, click" of the wheels on the track as the train chugs slowly by. I think of my conversation with the hobos and contemplate grabbing my bike and jumping on board. It's enticing, but there's no way I can pull all my belongings together before the train has eased through the area and silence descends again.

Like most camping experiences, noises are magnified, so it sounds like a gunshot when my next-door neighbor unzips his tent. My radar goes up. I hear the crunch of his feet on the turf. Then another unzipping sound. Then a loud rush of water. He's watering one of the trees. I smile. He farts loudly, and it's all I can do not to start roaring with laughter, like when you had the giggles in grade school in the library and you knew you weren't supposed to laugh. He grunts and trudges back to his tent, zips it up, and I hear him snoring soon thereafter.

I stop in Boise, Idaho. Our family has been invited to a wedding in Houston, and I find a hotel room, store my bike with a local bike shop, buy a six pack of 16-oz Rainier beer, and ice it down in my motel room sink. The first pull tastes like the best beer in the world. I slop it down far too quickly and place a collect call back to Scott Norgaard in Denver as I'm starting to feel loopy.

"How's it going man?"

"David, there's some guy named Tony who was just camping in my backyard."

"Are you serious?"

"Yeah, he said he met you down in Arkansas and has been tracking you ever since."

"I can't believe he's still following me. Let him know I'm up in Boise, Idaho. I'm storing my bike for a few days and flying down to Houston for a family wedding. I don't have any future address where he could meet up with me, but I'll be taking Highway 20 from Ontario (OR) up into eastern Oregon if you want to let him know. Maybe he'll find me."

"Got it."

After hanging up, I think to myself, "This is too wild. I hope Tony makes it up here. It'd be too cool to ride together."

The Houston wedding reintroduces me to the chaos of modern American cities, the traffic seemingly wedged together no matter where we drive in the car. Horns honk. People seem harried, distressed, angry, rude. While the wedding is fun, and I find I can still fit into my dad's suit (he and Mom bring one along for me to wear), I can't wait to get back on the road.

There are more wide-open spaces heading north and west out of Boise to Ontario, then through potato fields that seem to stretch forever. I decide to push myself through this portion of

Idaho

the trip, upping my daily mileage. At the beginning of the trip, I had a few days around 100 miles, then many where the ride was 60-70 a day, then slowly inching upwards to 120-130 miles a day as I got in better shape and it was no longer crucial to get to the next town.

Now I decide to hit 150 miles in a day. It's not such a great idea. Physically I can do it. Mentally and psychologically, it's another story.

I've slowly been losing weight, my body rock hard from all the work and probably not enough calories. I've heard potatoes have all the nutrients you need, so I decide to buy one and eat it as my energy carbohydrates for the day. This is another one of my not-so-good ideas. I pull the potato out while riding late in the afternoon. My mind is already in its altered daily state to keep from going crazy. I'm singing songs. I'm talking to the cows.

When I take a few bites from the raw potato, I think to myself, "This sucks. What am I doing? I'm in the middle of nowhere, going nowhere, coming from nowhere with all these potato fields around me. That doesn't mean I should be eating a raw potato." Though I finish crunching it up in my mouth, chewing thoroughly, and swallowing, it's the last time I'm going to eat a raw potato. Another lesson for the ages: Don't eat raw potatoes. Plus, they make you hallucinate (particularly if you have been on the road in the middle of nowhere bicycling for 150 miles and you're short on water). My mind drifts away like it's detached from my body, almost like I'm floating above myself, able to look down and watch my actions. I know this is not happening, but the potato, 150-mile day, and parched landscape all combine to contribute to my mind going down that path.

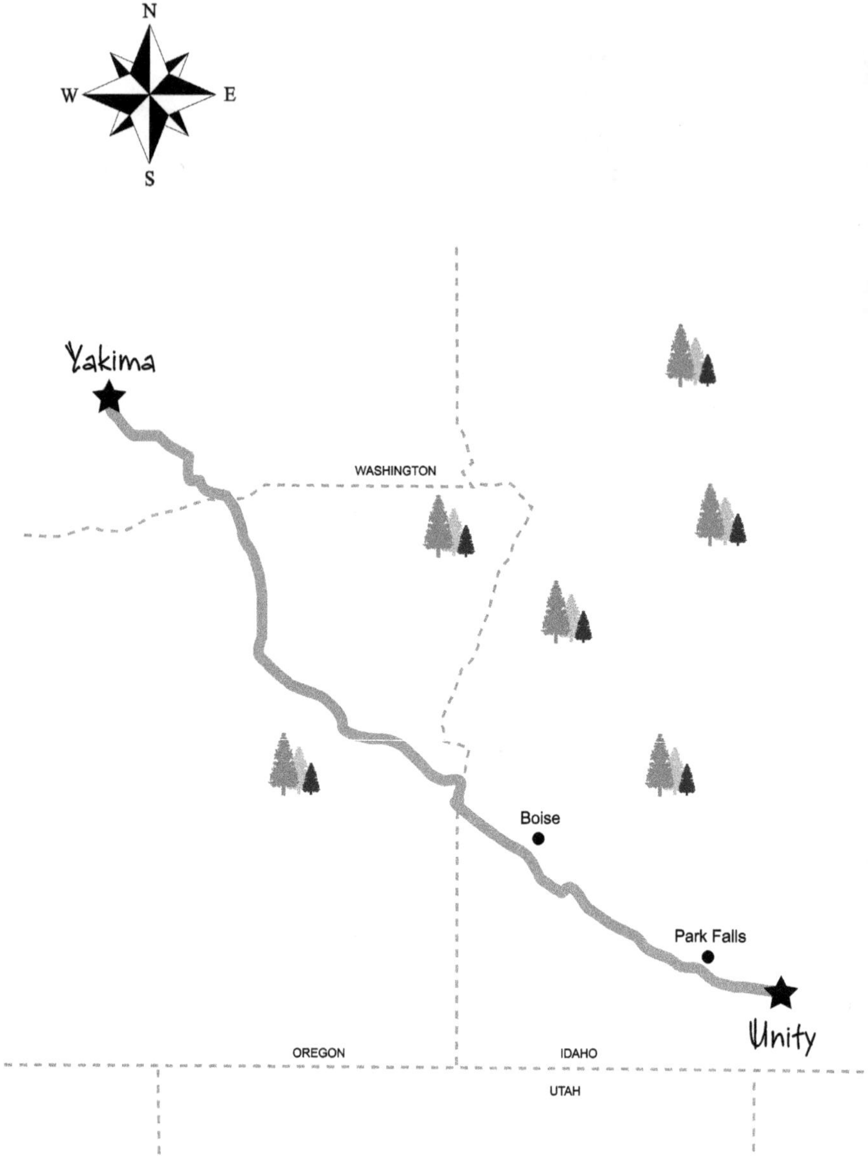

N
W
E
S
Yakima
WASHINGTON
Boise
Park Falls
Unity
OREGON
IDAHO
UTAH

Chapter 10
Thinning Apples

I had never been to Oregon. Seeing the Pacific Northwest and their people was one of my reasons for doing this trip. Their reputation of innovative thinking, outdoors culture, and hip happenings motivate me to follow the terrain and meet the locals.

Eastern Oregon surprises me as I stop to get my state map. Though I had no preconceived notions of what the landscape would look like, I didn't expect this: high and dry, desert-like, brown. The towns sit far apart and hold tiny populations. Then nothing for miles and miles. Scrub trees sprout here and there. I wind my way west.

For most of the trip, I've had no further issues with drivers. You adapt to hearing cars and trucks approaching from behind. You come to recognize the size and speed. Your eyes constantly edge over your back left shoulder to pay attention.

There's a vortex of wind that occurs when the vehicle blows by. You get sucked into it and must steady your bike. This, too, you grow accustomed to.

Particularly as I hit the western part of the U.S., cars tend to give me a wide berth. Drivers wave, give me the thumbs up, talk to me when I stop to get water and food at gas stations and supermarkets, except for one brief moment as I cross from Oregon into Washington. The road has a steep slide off to the right. I'm focused, dialed-in to avoiding certain death.

Then a pickup truck is on me. It zooms as close as possible, driving at highway speed, and attempts to nudge me while the driver honks. Startled, I begin to lose balance. I feel the front wheel shaking.

I look to my left and see two teenage boys laughing and pointing. Then they blast off. I right the bicycle, pull over, and look down into the abyss where I could have died because of adolescent male stupidity. I remember some of the shit I did as a teenager, and while I understood their behavior, I wish I could have caught them to teach them a lesson about how easily they could have killed someone and how horribly that could alter the trajectory of their lives.

***

I take Highway 26 across the state east to west, then head north on 197 through rolling hills and small towns. The air is dry, the sky bright, and traffic light. I pace myself towards Mount Hood National Forest and the Columbia River.

There's little wind for the most part, then I hit the Columbia. Whoa. I'm stunned by the scene – tons and tons of windsurfers. I've never seen windsurfing in person, and the vibrant colors of the sails sparkle as riders hop and shoot across the river, like human versions of salmon spawning upriver. I stop and stare, marveling at the athleticism and the wind tunnel created here.

I parallel the river briefly on 14, then head north up to 97 and Yakima through the edge of the Yakima Indian Reservation. The landscape is barren, depressing, and desolate. I'm running extremely low on money. Time to stop and earn some cash.

I've spoken off and on with local residents and understand that I can walk on and get a job at almost any apple orchard and work for a couple of weeks to make enough money to finish the trip. Sure enough, the first orchard I stop at hires me. Dave and Sarah run the place. They have two kids, and a teenager from Seattle named Matt is staying with them for the summer to work the orchard as well.

I get the impression they open their home to a teenage worker or two for the summer if they have a connection to the family. It's not something they would advertise, but they need workers every summer and use any means necessary to network and find them.

Though they don't openly talk about it, my sense is Matt has some problems with drugs, and his parents shipped him out to Dave and Sarah's to get him away from influencers in Seattle so hopefully he cleans up his act. He's a good guy, a bit moody, but helpful in showing me the ropes.

We had a huge apple orchard with multiple varieties behind our house in northern New Jersey, where I grew up. My brothers and I played there all the time, climbing trees, getting chased away by the owner. This orchard is different.

The trees are much smaller and closer together. It's thinning season. I've never heard of this before, despite feeling like I have some knowledge of the apple life cycle. Because so many apples crop up when budding begins, to make sure the apples reach a good size and get the nutrients needed, those working the orchard "thin" the apples. By hand, we pop off two apples if there is a cluster of three, remove three apples if it's a cluster of four. This allows more sap to reach the apples left on the tree. They grow bigger and juicier. The ground becomes littered with premature apples, which saddens me for some unknown reason.

Walking across the matted grass the first day, I'm not sure what to expect. The trees are smaller than I remember from my childhood, the limbs bent and laden with maturing green apples. I figure I'll pull apples with some other workers each day.

My first day requires a lesson. The orchard has a foreman who is a U.S. citizen. There is the Seattle teenager, myself, and about fifty other workers. All the rest are Mexican or Korean and don't have citizenship. We don't get apples to eat in the U.S. without this labor. Unemployment is fairly high in the U.S. in 1982. I ask the farmer why more Americans don't work for him. He says, "They won't come out here and work hard for $5.50 an hour."

Every day I'm impressed with the workers. They're tireless, never slowing down, working hard from seven in the morning till five in the afternoon, not complaining, seeming to enjoy themselves day after day as they share stories with each other.

There are three visibly pregnant women in the group. They are up and down the ladders all day long along with everyone else, singing and telling stories. At lunch, they pull out miniature burners to fire up tostados, tacos, and burritos. It smells great. The laughing and smiles are infectious.

Though the work is not hard, you must stay with it. There's no slacking. The foreman never has to remind anyone; I just keep pulling away at the baby apples. Sometimes I stand or use the ladder to get up higher. If I tire, I sit on the ground and thin the lowest apples on the trees to get my stamina back. Like the bike journey, there's a lesson about pacing yourself. I apply that lesson here, and it helps me get through the days when I feel like I can't pop one more apple off its stem. I shoulder on.

My high school Spanish comes back quickly, and it doesn't take long for my conversational skills to follow. Given the frequency of one verb used repeatedly by the men, I learn how to how to quickly conjugate chingar into chingamos, chingandos, and chinga. You can figure out what it means in English. The foreman says it's "muy malo" (very bad), the guy who acts as the head of the workers says it's "muy bueno" (very good). I laugh at how they look at the word differently.

Then, one day, they are all gone. The orchard is empty. It's me, the foreman, and the young guy from Seattle. I ask the foreman what happened. "U.S. immigration raid," he replies.

The workers knew beforehand and disappeared for the day. There's a network for the word to get out, so they won't be deported. The next day, everyone is back, working hard, but the tone of their voices is more subdued. No one was caught and deported, but they know the possibility lurks daily.

***

Dave and Sarah plan to be gone one Sunday, and I suggest that I'll cook Sunday dinner when they return. Chili is one of my specialties, and they agree. Matt tells me to make it hot, so I buy some red peppers, something I've never done before. This, of course, is a massive mistake.

The house smells great when they return, simmering meat, onions, and chili powder permeating the air. I make a salad and warm some bread, then taste the sauce and decide to add some extra chili powder and the red chilies. I taste again and toss some more in. Seems okay.

We all sit down, bless the meal, then dig in. I shovel a big spoonful and instantly grab my water and gulp down the entire glass. Yikes. I look around the table. Everyone either stuffs bread in the face, nibbles on the salad, or, like me, pounds water. Within seconds, water trickles down my armpits from the heat of the chili. I am so embarrassed. Everyone says how great it tastes, but after a couple of halfhearted bites, no one consumes any more, instead filling up on bread and salad. What a total culinary disaster.

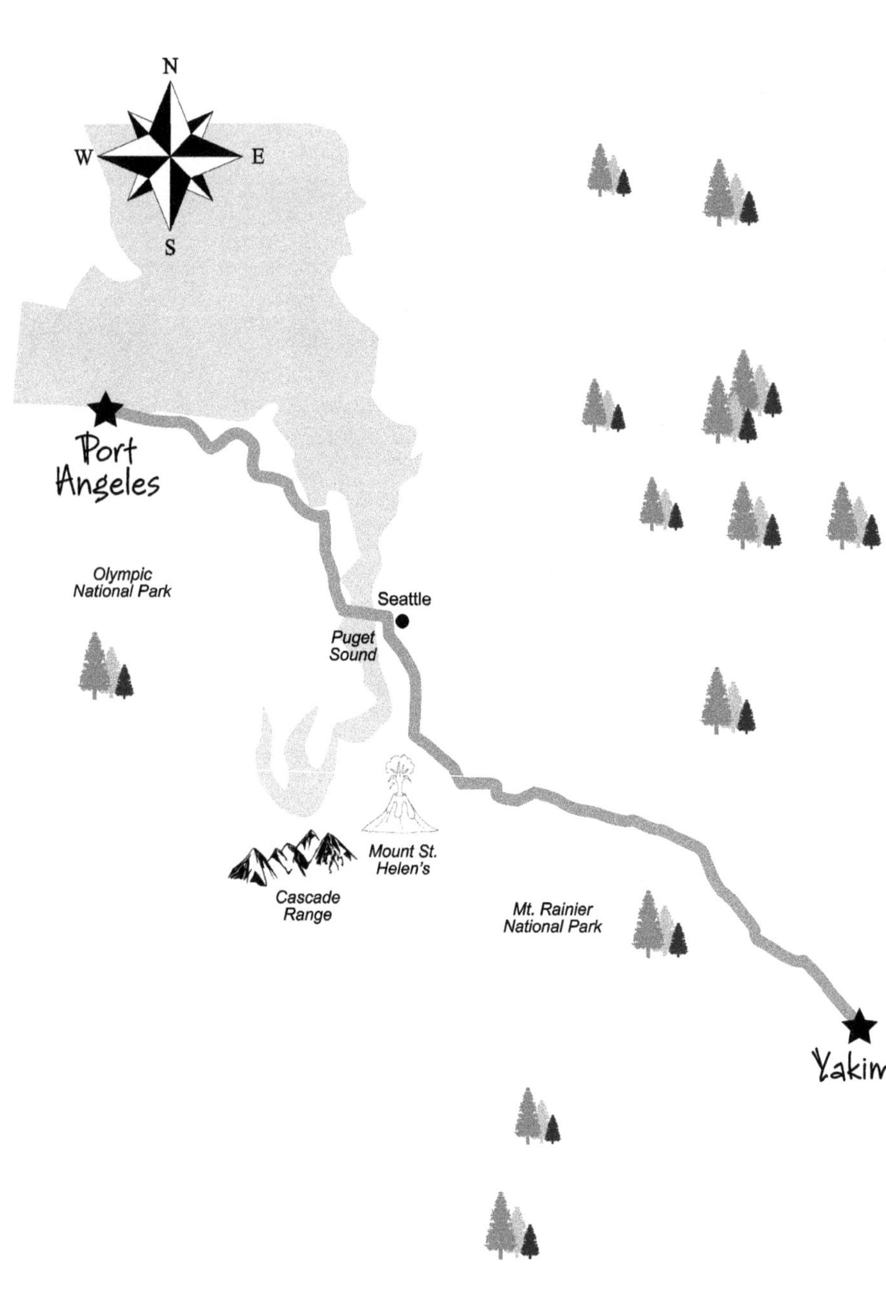
N
W
E
S
Port Angeles
Olympic National Park
Seattle
Puget Sound
Mount St. Helen's
Cascade Range
Mt. Rainier National Park
Yakim

Chapter 11
The Cascades, Mount St. Helens, and Seattle

I spend two weeks with Dave and Sarah, just long enough to make $550, which will hopefully carry me through the next three weeks or so to get home. In addition to making money, the work helps me recuperate and rest my body.

Not long after leaving Yakima on a gorgeous July morning, I head up to White Pass in the Cascade Range. I have a morbid desire to see the devastation wreaked by Mount St. Helens, which erupted two years earlier. I expect at the peak of the pass I will be able to easily see what Mother Nature wrought.

Almost no traffic on the way. Pine trees line the highway. Much of the day I spend in silence. So silent in fact that I can feel the shudder of cars approaching either from the west or behind me from the east, an eerie sensation. As I pedal, I sense rhythm from the earth. With no traffic, there is solely the hum of my tires. Then I feel a slight pulse.

I have no idea at first what the pulse signals, then after it occurs several times, I realize it signifies that a vehicle is approaching. It must have been 3-4 miles away because it emerged in three to four minutes after I initially sensed the vibrations through my bicycle frame.

You come to understand how the Native Americans could

feel large buffalo herds approaching. Their weight, like the automobile, must have made the earth shake.

I'm still ascending to the pass when I feel the ground shudder ahead. Nothing in sight. I stop and listen. I can feel something is close, but I don't know what. My spider sense tingles.

Suddenly, two huge deer leap from the trees and land on the road just in front of me. They look around and plod up the highway, then disappear back into the woods. I marvel at their size, grace, and power.

Above: the Cascades
Left: Mount St. Helens

The weather stays good until right near the top of White Pass when it gets foggy from snow in the higher elevations, and my view becomes completely blocked. I'm pissed. It stays this way as I start down the west side of the range. Still no Mount St. Helens. Finally, the mountain emerges as if the sun suddenly rose. I look down and see trees laying by the thousands, looking like toppled matchsticks. The vista of destruction seems to stretch forever. But new growth has already started, just two years after the eruption. Green is noticeable everywhere. Mother Earth mending herself.

***

The rest of the ride into Seattle proves uneventful, though I do catch up with a local bicyclist who offers me a place to stay at his house with him and his wife. Jim is about 50, and a Seattleite by birth. He shares some history of the area and places for me to see. He's a wiry guy, balding and totally laid back, a consummate bicyclist who rides everywhere rather than driving. That makes him a hero to me and someone I want to get to know better. I figure he'll be a great resource.

First, I visit Tom, whom I met earlier in the trip at Dinosaur National Monument. Both he and Jim live up near the University of Washington, north of the core downtown. I'm welcomed with open arms and a superb homegrown meal made with ingredients from his garden. Tom composts all discarded fruits and vegetables, creating an amazing nutrient-rich environment for the veggies he grows. He's not a professional chef, but his cooking sure tastes like he is.

Like others on the trip, Tom opens his door to me, offers a spare bedroom, and lets me stay as long as I'd like to recuperate and see the area. He too gives me a rundown of the area, and the fish market and Space Needle make up the agenda for the next day.

Seattle in July dazzles me. There's a lightness to the air which makes everything sparkle and lends vibrancy to the city. The local downtown market buzzes with activity. Fresh local food abounds. The fish market provides live entertainment as the men call out orders and toss huge salmon to each other to slice and deliver to customers. They never drop one while I watch this mesmerizing show. Makes me wonder if I could catch a slick fish.

I follow the market with a stop at the Space Needle, taking the elevator to the top and soaking in the 360-degree view. To the west lies Puget Sound. The city unfolds below. The most remarkable recognition occurs when I realize how much water fills the area. Lakes abound. Take that, Minnesota and Wisconsin. You read about how much it rains in Seattle. The summer months though are sunny, and I've arrived at the perfect time to stay out of the drizzle and in 70-degree sunny days.

I bike up to Jim's to spend the next few days with him and his wife. His house has a deck with an epic view of Puget Sound. We crack open beers and reminisce on the trip. He's covered much of the Pacific Northwest as an avid biker and offers multiple suggestions for places to see.

The next day, we tour the University of Washington and

some other sites near his home. Jim gives me the lowdown on how to get around and where to go next, which involves a ferry ride across Puget Sound, then north to Port Angeles. Originally, I had hoped to spend some significant time in the Olympic Mountains in the far northwest part of Washington but decide to head to the San Juan Islands instead, per Jim's suggestion.

Once across Puget Sound, the area reminds me of small beach towns with cottages. Many people commute daily across the sound to Seattle, and the prices of these places are rising astronomically from what I'm told.

Arriving at the ferry, I find a bike offers a massive advantage. I don't have to wait in line. I'm allowed to walk my bike right up to the front and get on the next ferry. Ahoy, mateys!

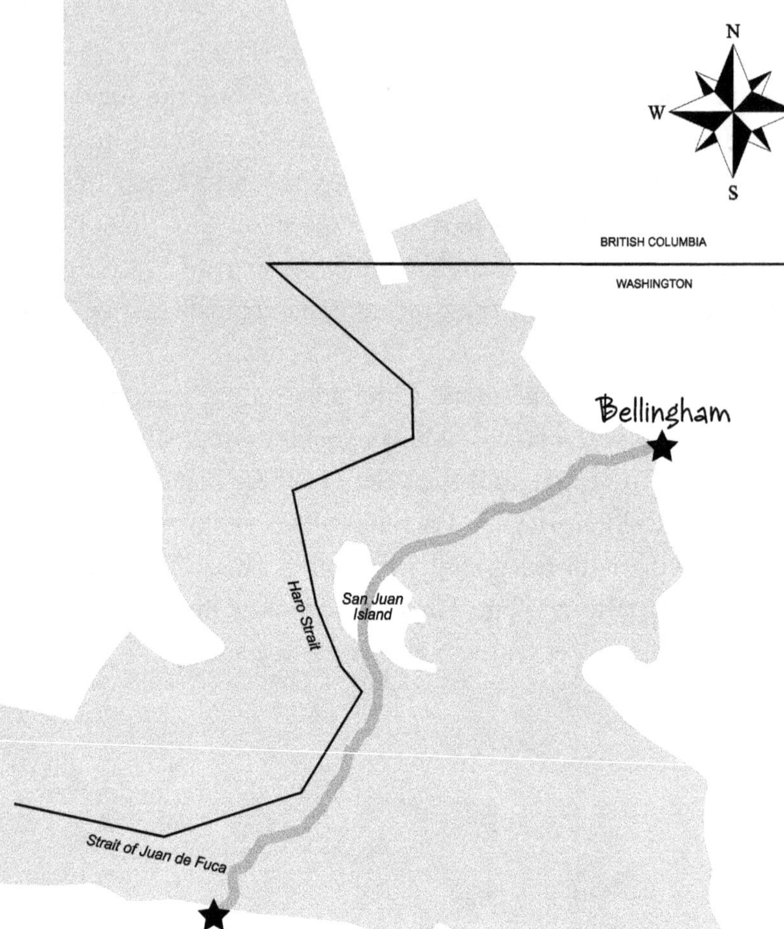
N
W
E
S
BRITISH COLUMBIA
WASHINGTON
Bellingham
Haro Strait
San Juan
Island
Strait of Juan de Fuca
Port
Angeles
Olympic
National Park

Chapter 12
The San Juan Islands

The open sea beckons. The streak of blue sky continues and the sun shimmers as the ferry departs from Port Angeles.

I know nothing about the San Juan Islands. Multiple people have told me I need to ride around them, so here I go.

The first stop isn't much. There's a store and a couple of buildings where we land, then rough scrub and isolation as I pedal to the tip of the island. I finally reach the end of the road late that afternoon, and the ocean opens up panoramically in front of me.

Off to the east, people mill about at some kind of event. I ride over to check out the scene. Everyone is dressed up – for a wedding! Seeing tuxedos and bridal dresses out here in the middle of nowhere is pretty wild. I wonder how they chose the site. They'll remember the ceremony forever, for sure. This is a small-moneyed affair, no question, when you look at the attendees – incredibly well-dressed and groomed, good-looking. They are mostly on the younger side, probably under thirty-five, and the positive vibe is palpable as they wait for the ceremony to begin, talking in small groups with visible energy.

Having been on the road for close to three months now, I've grown accustomed to finding places to sleep by the side of the road – picnic areas, town parks, or even just finding a spot of woods to pitch my tent away from the road. There's a small roadside rest area with a good grassy space that I select tonight. No cars go by. I drift off.

The silence is broken by the crunching of sticks in the woods. Instantly, I'm alert, listening closely, trying to figure it out.

A twig cracks. I wait. No noise.

Then I hear soft steps. I tense.

Then silence.

My ears strain.

More steps. Something heavy. What the heck?

I work through my fear and then realize a deer has come foraging.

I don't even unzip my tent. I can tell by the steps, and then I can actually hear-munching food. The quiet of the night in the wild.

***

The next island offers much the same as the first, a few more buildings where the ferry arrives, a small restaurant, lots of tourists. People have canoes and kayaks attached to their vehicles. Everyone is friendly and helpful.

I leave and again pedal to the end of the island. There's a path down to the ocean, so I carry my bike down, then meander to the edge of the water. This is whale watching territory, but I don't see any. It's a disappointment after spending time at the ocean's edge, soaking in the sights, scanning the deep sea relentlessly for water spouting or a titanic splash. Oh well, sometimes you don't get to see what you'd hoped, and sometimes you get an unexpected experience, like the wedding.

The current of the ocean pulses and flows by at an astounding speed. I had no idea ocean currents move like that, akin to a fast-flowing river.

Seaweed-like giant snakes flutter in the water. Their movement shows how fast the water around them is moving. I imagine if you jumped in the water, you'd be whipped hundreds of yards away in a minute.

There's a massive purple starfish stuck to the top of a rock just below the surface of the water as I walk along the shore. I've never seen a purple starfish before. Didn't even know they existed. This creature is close to two feet in diameter. I wonder if starfish can be eaten.

Island life is funky and slow. No one rushes. Cars move lazily. Good for letting the mind drift.

The ferry rides further relax me. I write, read, gaze at the spectacular vistas. The people of the ferry are excited and plugged into the environment around them.

***

Returning to the U.S. mainland just outside Bellingham, Washington, I'm back into pine forest. Huge trees, hills, brilliant skies, and clean air. I head down a hill and catch up with some local bikers. They haul. I barely can keep up, but finally establish a pace and open a conversation with a bearded man who explains where to go in Bellingham.

The city turns out to be a throwback to the hippie era, with lots of long hair, flower skirts, and tie-dyed shirts. The biker directs me to a local café for breakfast, and I find it easily downtown.

Inside is warm and inviting. Rough-hewn wood ceiling, small and intimate, waitresses with engaging manners and wide smiles. A guitarist plays folks songs. Lots of chattering around the tables and a ruddy look on everyone's faces. I order breakfast and coffee, a big treat for me, and eat with gusto, enjoying the music and just sitting in comfort.

A cup of coffee is a luxury. It's been a while. Time for a real breakfast. I get my standard omelet, cheese and onion, and wolf down the toast and jam as the guitarist plugs away, quietly singing a folk song. I could live here.

Buzzed on the sudden caffeine, I decide to wind through town, the hippie vibe evident in the local population. Lots of long hair on the men. Peasant dresses on the women. Hippie beads. Sandals with no socks.

Racing and touring bikes cruise the streets. It seems to be standard fare in the Pacific Northwest that you'll see more bicycles, kayaks, canoes, and other outdoor gear packed on cars. Mount Baker sits to the east of Bellingham, part of the upper Cascade Range, and the north edge of the Puget Sound frames the western edge of the city. Western Washington University is in Bellingham, further contributing to a youthfulness in the area and its eco-friendly atmosphere. The sky is a perfect, cloudless blue for the days I'm there. It all makes you want to come back.

After my casual tour to get a better feel for Bellingham, it's off to Canada next.

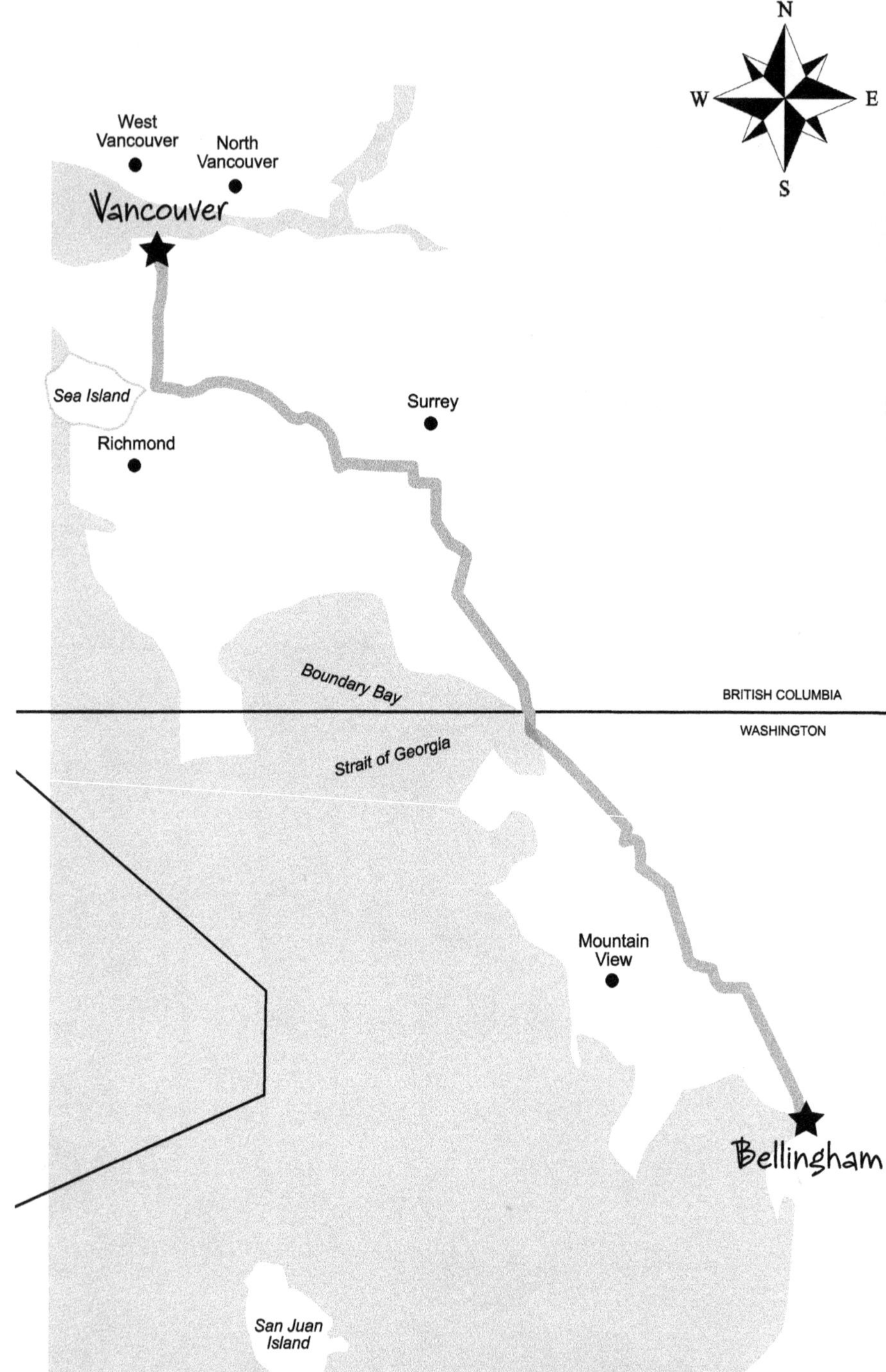
N
W
E
S
West Vancouver
North Vancouver
Vancouver
Sea Island
Surrey
Richmond
Boundary Bay
BRITISH COLUMBIA
WASHINGTON
Strait of Georgia
Mountain View
Bellingham
San Juan Island

Chapter 13
Diversity in Vancouver

The land heading up to the Canadian border flies in the face of my preconceived notions and is mostly flat farm acreage. Temperatures hover in the low 70s, no breeze, the air liquid. Bicycling heaven.

I feel slightly apprehensive approaching the border, probably due to interacting with law enforcement personnel, this time with someone from another country. You worry.

The border patrol agent eyes my bike and gives me a mean stare. Perusing my driver's license, he asks me, "What's your name? Where are you from? Why are you visiting Canada?"

I feel like he thinks I'm leading the insurrection or something. I answer openly. "Riding my bicycle across the U.S. and Canada. I'll probably be here for two weeks or so."

He looks at me intently, then examines the contents of my front and back saddle bags along with the plastic bag used to encase the tent and sleeping bag. Nothing unusual in there, or so I think.

He nudges all the items around and immediately drills down to a canister. "What's this?"

It comes across as an "Aha" moment, like he's found the thing to challenge me with and prevent me from crossing over.

"Uh, a canister of pepper spray. One of my female friends gave it to me for safety when I left Milwaukee."

He eyes me like I'm lying. "You can't bring this with you into the country."

Rather than ask why not, I nod my head. "Okay."

He grabs it and puts it into a container as if he's found a jewel and justified his job. He rummages some more, but his heart doesn't appear to be in it. Finishing up, I get ready to hop on the bike when he stops me. "What's your name?"

I look at him oddly. "Dave Simon."

He nods, like I've confirmed something. "Am I free to go?" He nods again.

Welcome to Canada.

***

I'm heading to the big city – Vancouver – and some international flavor. It doesn't disappoint.

I'm staying with a friend of a friend of my parents. They live in a bungalow out by the English Bay, tall pines overshadowing the neighborhood, a sense of quiet permeating the area. We catch up on the trip as I share stories and explore the beach, rest, eat some home-cooked food, and start considering where I am and what's next.

The journey's end has started to creep into my mind. There are only so many days left before classes begin in the fall – two to three weeks to get back to Milwaukee, and a bit more than a week after that, classes start. Though I've put school out of

Family I stayed with in Vancouver

my mind, occasionally it sneaks back in, and I know I'll have to gear up to take a couple of finals that were postponed so I could leave the city back in May. I push those thoughts back to stay the course on the next steps and the best way to get across southern Canada, from British Columbia to Manitoba.

I'm not going to have time to bike all the way back across Canada. I consider options. The most sensible solution means taking the trans-Canadian train for portions of the trip.

Coming across the U.S. east to west, the Kansas-eastern Colorado portion of the country was the flattest, least inviting, and was scenically uninteresting. You don't think about something like that until you consider going back over the same type of territory, only hundreds of miles to the north. That section of Canada is flat, the small towns far apart. I file it away in the back of my head on how to best eliminate those miles.

But next is still exploring Vancouver, perhaps the most international city I've ever visited. My hosts and I head downtown one evening for dinner. Walking the streets, I'm struck by language. I start to count. Within minutes, I add up eight languages I've heard. Some are identifiable, others not. But French, German, Chinese, Spanish, Japanese, Russian, and Indian dialect all jump out. As we continue to walk, other groups meander by, and snippets of their native tongue add to the flavor of diversity.

The restaurants reflect this diversity, and despite the crowded nature of the downtown area, there is no stress or pushiness. People converse. They give you room. They engage with each other.

I'm struck by the friendliness in the face of multiple cultures. There is a sense of togetherness despite the diversity. The city, too, is exquisitely clean, the skyline magnificent. I've been to other Canadian cities, and Vancouver reinforces a sense of pride in its country. The streets are spotless, unlike the trash you see regularly around U.S. cities. It's almost like they've taken a hose and washed all the trash away. I wish people who live in U.S. cities would take a lesson from this.

The entire area is lush. Later in the week, we hike over a huge gorge, giving me a touch of what is to come – the Canadian Rockies. The canyon reveals an awe-inspiring drop into the river below. I wonder what the Rockies will hold for me and decide to start the trip east on the train to store energy for the final stretch. I head to the train station to check my bicycle in.

Vancouver, British Columbia

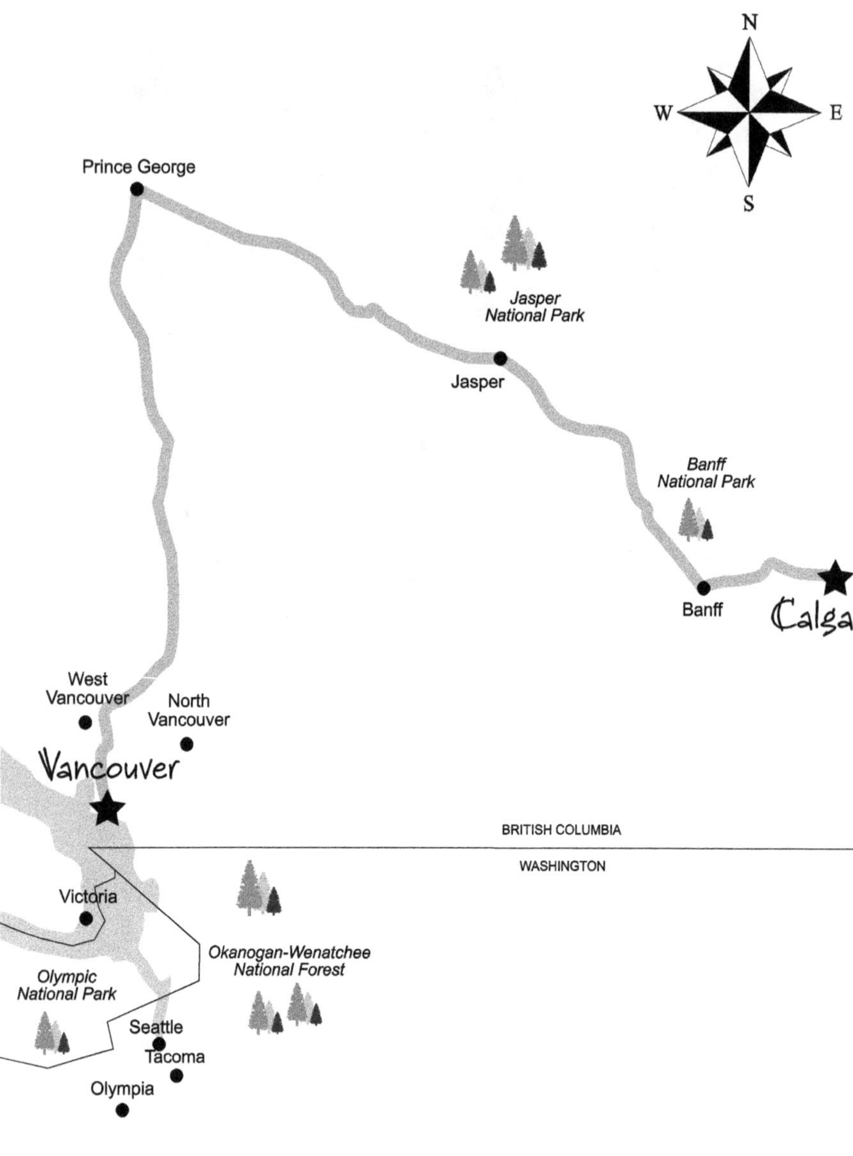

N
W
E
S
Prince George
Jasper National Park
Jasper
Banff National Park
Banff
Calgary
West Vancouver
North Vancouver
Vancouver
BRITISH COLUMBIA
WASHINGTON
Victoria
Okanogan-Wenatchee National Forest
Olympic National Park
Seattle
Tacoma
Olympia

Chapter 14
The Canadian Rockies

Though the U.S. and Canada are much alike, I find a few contrasts. Even with all the kindness and caring I received across the U.S., there is an even greater sense of comfort and international flavor that is inviting in Canada. They seem to encourage travel, and I sense this is due to their being so far north that many of them want to go somewhere during the winter to warm up, and the only place to do this is in another country. So they travel. And they accept that other people travel and want to see their country.

Checking my bicycle demonstrates an example of one difference between the two countries. In the U.S., you must box your bicycle to ship it by rail. In Vancouver, I just check my bike. Simple. Done. I buy my ticket, get on the train. People expect bicyclists here, so they make it easy for you to get on and off to explore the country.

There was an option for a deluxe seat. That wasn't in the budget. I park my sore butt in a tough leather seat instead, but there's enough room for four people, so I can stretch out, sleep, and read. We slowly lurch out of the station, the railcars bumping side to side as the city recedes and we ascend into the base of the west side of the Rockies. The train cannot go fast.

It's too steep, so there is a lot of time to look out the window and marvel in the splendor of the forest and how much land out there remains untouched. We snake slowly, eventually establishing a steady pace, but nowhere near what you get in terms of speed on the open prairie. We chug along at 25, 30, sometimes 40 mph.

A young backpacking Canadian couple comes into my car, and they plop their gear down in the seats next to mine. We quickly start sharing stories. They backpacked overseas and are now exploring more of their own country. Their enthusiasm infects me. They've spent most of the summer outdoors, and I'm struck by the rugged nature of their features, the sunburned glint to their skin, and how alive their eyes are. It's a look I've seen frequently over the summer in people who spend a lot of time outdoors, and I wonder if I too come across this way to others. Has some of the kindness I've received been based on how people perceive me and my openness?

The couple knows the Rockies well, and based on their suggestion, I make the decision to get off the train in Jasper, then bike down to Calgary, and back on the train from there across the plains of Canada. The plan makes sense to allow exploration of the mountains, while minimizing the trek of the flatlands, and gives me enough time to head down from Winnipeg, into Minnesota, and back to Wisconsin.

In the middle of the night, we make our first stop: Prince George, British Columbia, the farthest point north I've ever been in my life, and I choose to disembark, get my bike, and ride around. The train does not leave again until late in the day, and we've been deposited early in the morning.

The city has a population of over 65,000, but it seems more like 20,000 with a small-town feel. There are two distinct commercial sections, one more oriented to restaurants and one for shopping.

I head into town on this Sunday morning to grab some food. Downtown is dead, quiet enough to hear the flies buzz. A slight breeze ripples through the one block area. Every shop is closed. A newspaper sheet scuttles by and launches into the air. Eerie.

There's a two-block area that appears to house most of the retail establishments with your basic national stores interspersed with local shops – jewelry, leather, and touristy knickknack places. It's quaint with very little foot traffic this morning.

Walking the strip, a local member of the tribe from the area, based on his looks, snoozes on a park bench. Another guy saunters down the street, stumbling, stopping and looking in windows. When he comes closer, I smell the booze and realize he is either still drunk from the night before or started drinking early in the morning. It's not even noon, and he's soon unconscious.

I decide to get out of the main block and head back closer to the train station, grabbing a hearty bacon, egg, and potato breakfast and taking my time eating it before re-embarking on the train after 10 p.m., when it's still light here in the land of the midnight sun. The longer exposure to daylight heightens your energy and messes with your head, making you think there's no need for sleep and that you should still be doing something productive well past your normal bedtime.

***

Jasper is a tourist town that I decide not to experience. I get off the train and begin my descent down the Rockies eastward. The mostly downhill ride provides a welcome change when your mind thinks you're been biking uphill all summer. That was not the case, but the psychology of the trip eats at you that way, and you have to conquer those negative thoughts or you'll never finish.

In Jasper, I bump into a guy after getting off the train who's on a short biking excursion, heading down to Banff. Securing my gear and orienting myself, we chat for a bit and decide to pair up. Since splitting up with Randy, I've been on my own, and it feels good to have someone to talk with as we trade places breaking the wind. He's on a two-week trip, taking off from his job.

On the second day out of Jasper, a lightning storm hits, one of the craziest experiences of my life. Given our altitude, the sensation feels like being inside the lightning.

One minute, the sky is clear. Then a bolt slams the ground next to us and rattles our bikes. We keep pedaling. I look up at the sky and see blue and one or two clouds. Weird. How does something like this happen?

We ride hard, zipping around curves, thunder rumbling,

and another bolt hits behind the mountain to our east. It's not a slamming, rattling feeling. More like a pop and crackle like a forest fire. I can taste the electricity in the air.

I'm frightened, but my Canadian biking buddy shoulders on, apparently used to this, pushing himself harder down the mountain. I follow his lead, hitting the curves at high speeds, sliding behind in his slipstream. A few more flashes follow off in the trees to our west, then suddenly it's gone. As rapidly as the electrical bursts started, they leave. And oddly, no rain.

We speed our way to Banff. Whether it is the threat of what we just rode through or wanting to get to town and have a roof over our heads, I'm unsure. But he rides hard, and I do my best to follow.

When you establish a rhythm touring on your bicycle, there's a pace around 12-13 mph that is steady. Cranking that average speed up more than that feels out of the comfort range. We're way out of that range.

I break a sweat and feel myself going beyond my abilities to stay with him, getting the sense that suddenly he wants to leave me behind. I'm not sure exactly why I feel this way. Maybe it's that he's a much faster rider than me, and I'm dialed into pedaling at a slower, steady pace, and he's throwing me off that. Whatever the reason, I have to push myself harder and harder to keep him in sight.

Banff explodes in front of us. WHOA! The most panoramic, breathtaking site of the trip, a wide expanse of green and fir trees revealed in a valley set against the backdrop of the vast Rockies. From our perch in the Rockies, we look down on this burst of colors. Greens like you've never seen before cover the fir trees that surround Banff. The Bow River winds its way through the bucolic valley, water sparkling and pristine. The buildings all look fresh and fit into the natural feel of the city in a way that makes you want to stay and spend extra time experiencing the local atmosphere. The bright sun gives it all a sharpness, framing the area in your mind so its vivid image stays with you long afterwards.

We fly into Banff, and I finally catch him, breathless. The plan was for me to crash at his place, a house he shares with several buddies. Suddenly though, he seems iffy about offering up shared quarters, the first this has happened on the trip. I have no place else to go. We keep talking. I appeal to his better side, and he agrees to let me stay one night.

The evening starts awkwardly, but after a few beers he warms up. The biking stories start to flow. Like war stories, we play off each other. His roommates come home from their day jobs, and we continue to dent their beer supply. Maybe he was concerned I would drink all his beer – a distinct possibility after the thirst I built up on the road. Hammered, I crash on the couch, waking the next morning to the only hangover of the trip.

I ride leisurely down to Calgary. The city is a northern Denver. Another tremendously clean Canadian city. I head to a city park to wait for my train departure and just lie around, soaking in the sun and the atmosphere of people out for a walk or on their lunch break. There's a sense of youth, possibility and positivity in the park, and I strike up a conversation with a young woman who describes how Calgary is attracting people from all across Canada who want to ski, backpack, hike, kayak, and canoe.

What she describes sounds striking similar to what is happening in the U.S. in Denver and smaller cities at the ridge of the Rockies – people moving there for lifestyle reasons and figuring out their jobs afterwards.

I've not had any romantic interactions on the trip, but my heart is tugged to stay. There's a train to catch, so with regret I leave with Calgary and the young woman etched into the trip's memories.

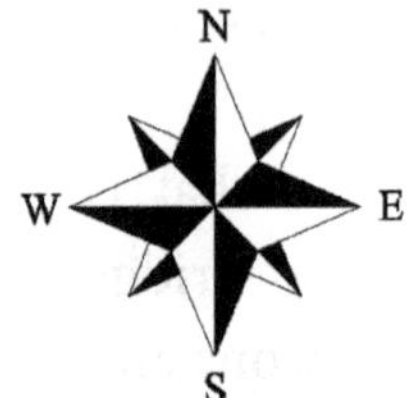

Poplar/Nanowin Rivers Park Reserve

Lake Winnipeg

Banff National Park

Calgary

Winnipeg

SASKATCHEWAN

Kootenal National Forest

MONTANA

NORTH DAKOTA

MINNESOTA

Flathead National Forest

Chapter 15
Alaskan Firefighter

As the train leaves the Calgary station to take me east to Winnipeg, I contemplate the hours ahead. Coming west across the plains of the U.S. was one of the least entertaining and most stressful parts of the trip. The terrain is similar in this part of Canada, so I doubt there will be much stand-out scenery. But it would have been fun to have prevailing winds at my back.

Looking at the map, there are funky-sounding towns ahead I'll be skipping as the train slides through the heartland of southern Canada – Medicine Hat, Swift Current, and Moose Jaw before we get to Regina. From there, even more openness beckons. I like my decision to sit back, read, and watch from the window as the countryside flies by at five times my normal biking speed.

A surprise enters the car in the form of a tall man with wavy dark hair and deeply sunburned skin. He's impressive, about 6'3", maybe taller, and a full backpack rides comfortably over his shoulders, like a friendly koala along for the ride. He looks like he's been out in the country for months. Turns out he has, but not in a way you would have imagined.

His smile spreads from Calgary to Winnipeg. He plunks down beside me, unleashes his belongings, and plops them on the ground before extending a mammoth hand in greeting to me. "I'm Allen."

"Dave. Pleased to meet you."

He can't get enough of my trip, asking questions, wanting to know where I've been, my favorite part of the trip (ferrying and biking the San Juan Islands and back into Bellingham). He listens intently, his eyes a beacon of interest. You don't meet people like this often – those whose deep care for others transcends their own statements and words.

He's been fighting fires in Alaska all summer, and now he's going home to Alabama to propose to his girlfriend. He shows me the ring. It's monumental. He's proud and obviously deeply in love.

Allen has been gone from Alabama for a couple of years. He didn't know what he wanted to do after high school. Wasn't headed to college or the military. No real job prospects in the small town where he grew up.

He wanted to be outdoors. Way outdoors. Ergo, Alaska.

He hitched on quickly with the fire service once he got to the state. There's ongoing need for young bodies to drop into the wilderness and live for weeks on end, working all day, every day, to put out fires. He loves the job.

They fly by helicopter and parachute in with the basics in terms of gear, a shovel being one of the most important tools they have to fight blazes. He and his teammates dig lines to try to stop fires from leaping deeper and deeper into the forest. Further provisions are dropped by plane or helicopter the longer the stay in the outback.

The danger of the job translates to good pay – enough to cover his trip home, the rock for his girlfriend, probably a blast of a honeymoon, and maybe even a set-aside for the two of them to get fully started in life together. His intensity and excitement are infectious as he relates the smoke and flames heading the way of the team and the speed and focus they must deliver or die in the process. He's on edge, his leg thumping as he talks about bringing down trees, running through fire walls, and protecting the wilderness from going up in smoke.

He works round-the-clock. With the fires recently letting, he's allowed to take off, catch a flight, then this train, then he'll hitchhike when he gets back to the U.S. to return to his fiancé and propose. The train will get him to the middle of Canada before he starts sticking his thumb out, a long haul seeking rides from strangers. Catching the energy that comes off him as we speak, I have no qualms that he'll make it. My own trip reassures me of the spirit in others that will make things happen.

Allen plans to have his girlfriend join him in Alaska. I don't doubt that will happen. I can't imagine anyone coming in contact with him and not following him. We become quick brothers, someone you'd go to war with. He'd have my back, and I'd have his. I imagine the fire team in the woods, the importance of the littlest things to ensure survival.

***

We talk long into the night. The train pulls into Winnipeg late at night, the city lights twinkling. Feels like we just left

Calgary. Allen hefts his backpack onto his shoulders like it's a bag of popcorn. As he lumbers off, I pick up my bicycle and wander on, once again renewed by the spirit of someone I've met along the way.

I walk around near the train station in the coming dawn with my saddlebags and bike, taking in the lights and quiet emptiness of the area. Wind pushes paper down the sidewalk. There's a Chinese restaurant across the street from the station.

As the sunrise paints the eastern sky, I head south and am out of the city landscape quickly, the land and road flat. Minnesota's on deck, then back to Wisconsin. I'm getting antsy.

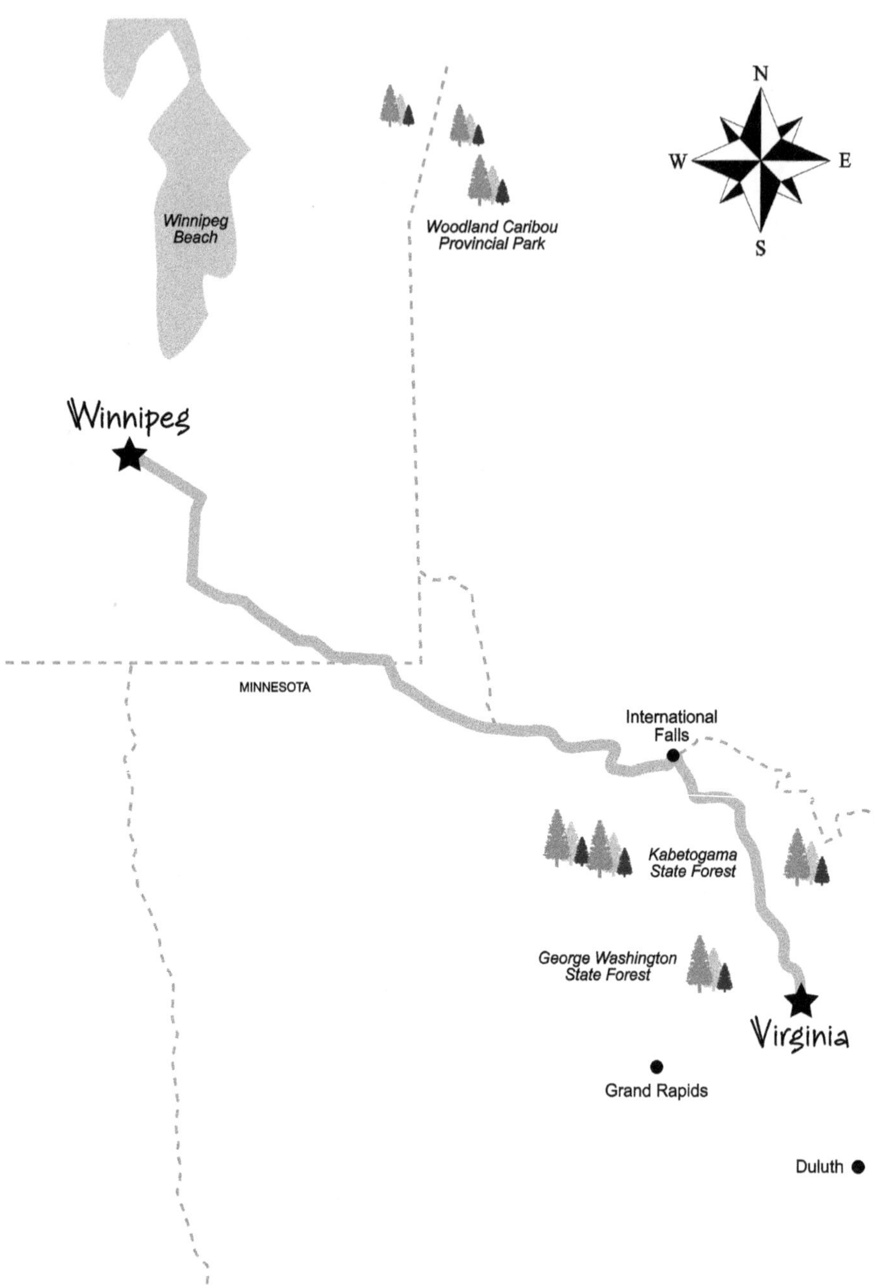
Winnipeg Beach
Woodland Caribou Provincial Park
N
W
E
S
Winnipeg
MINNESOTA
International Falls
Kabetogama State Forest
George Washington State Forest
Virginia
Grand Rapids
Duluth

Chapter 16
Returning to the U.S.

You'd think I'd be prepared for U.S. Customs as I reach International Falls, Minnesota, but I'm not. The agents try to stump me in this direction, too. They must think I have massive contraband inside my bicycle tires.

They do have a guy pulled over, and the agent tells me they've got him on a pot charge. You hear stories of this – people arrested for having small amounts of marijuana. I shake my head. Seems like there could a better use of time and money then hounding tourists for a bit of pot in their pockets.

The agent pulls out my meager belongings and dumps them on his table for inspection. I watch my apple bounce on the ground, roll under a car tire, and get squished. I look at him like, "What the fuck?", and he shrugs his shoulders, then begins sifting through my stuff, looking to hang something on me.

Once done, he offers me a peace orange. "Sorry about the apple. Here's an orange."

I'm not big on oranges, but what the heck, I'll take it. I start to put it into my front handlebar bag.

"Oh, you can't take it across the border like that."

"What do you mean?"

"The rind can have some kind of mite on it, so we don't allow it to cross the border."

"So why did you give it to me?"

"You can eat it now, if you'd like."

"I'm not hungry."

"You can peel it then and leave the peel with me, then take it into the U.S."

I look at him like he needs his head examined.

He shrugs.

I peel the orange, put the meat into the saddlebag, and pedal off.

***

Back in the U.S., there's not much change in scenery. Lots of slight undulations to the land and lakes off to the side. You have kind of the same syndrome when you cross state lines in the U.S., and you think suddenly it will be new terrain, but it's mostly a continuation from where you've just been. Land doesn't change dramatically, except in a couple of places, like the Rocky Mountains.

Minnesota proudly touts the state as The Land of 10,000 Lakes and, based on what I see, lives up to that reputation. Small scrub pine and birch trees abound as I pedal south through Kabetogama State Forest. Traffic is light. Cars give me a wide berth.

For most of the trip, I've stuck to my eating routine of granola and fruit and some protein like kippers or sardines.

Canned fish tastes amazing when you're famished. I'm not sure if this is the best diet, and I've stoked up on carbs whenever I've had the opportunity. What the diet does afford is light traveling. It doesn't take up much space. I can jam all my culinary delights easily into my saddlebags. I stop daily to resupply.

To keep costs down, I don't eat at restaurants. I decide to change that these last few days. Stop and take in the local dive.

The first day in Minnesota, I pull into a tavern near Orr, aka lumberjack country. The weather is cool for mid-August. The guy mopping the bar sports has a Bunyanesque beard and wears a red flannel shirt. He greets me heartily. There's one professional drinker at the bar with him, who nods a boozy greeting. Have I entered an LL Bean catalog gone awry?

Time for a greasy burger. I order a cheeseburger with the works, some fries, and splurge on a beer. It's a classic bar burger, oozing with grease, and I inhale it hungrily after dousing it with mustard and adding a tomato slice, raw onions, and soggy pickles. The fries are just out of the fryer, too hot to handle, and not being able to wait, I burn my mouth and down the beer to cool them off. Drinking booze and biking don't mix, but I feel like hanging out for a while and catching a few local stories, so I plan to stay until the fumes from the beer wear off.

This part of the state is economically depressed, according to the bartender. He shares with me that the tavern offers one place to work, but not much else is available unless you're an iron miner or in the logging business in some way. The towns have grown sparse as people graduate from high school and leave in search of their future.

But none of that tames the bartender's spirit. He's stayed in the community, cobbling together a few odd jobs, working for cash and making the big bucks tending bar. He mirrors a common story from the trip, particularly in the smaller out-of-the-way towns across North America. People move to the big cities to find jobs or meet someone of the opposite sex, or just to have more excitement. The cities expand. The isolated towns contract. I find this sad in many ways, yet the heart of America is here in the kindness people display, their warmth, and their spirit to do what they can to keep their hometown viable.

It makes you wish that we could find that middle ground in the United States – where the big cities didn't have to get so big and the small towns didn't have to shrivel into mere apparitions of their former selves. If we could have a bit of mixing between those two trends, the country would be much better off.

First, the horrific city traffic would decrease. Fewer cars on the road in urban areas could open things up for bicycles and walking areas. You can live close to your job and experience those extra particulars urban areas have to offer without feeling hemmed in by buildings, people, cars, and the expenses that occur when too many people try to relocate into one area.

Second, if smaller communities could retain a job base and some elements of cities in terms of culture, restaurants, medical care, and other amenities, a lot more people would be willing to remain where they are when graduating high school because a strong future would be available in the job market and for their outside interests.

But the trend moves relentlessly in the opposite direction.

That is evident as I've crossed the U.S. I'm not sure how to change the metamorphosis, except through viable business opportunities that create the types of jobs that attract people. I've found that many people who want to live away from others do so, like the bartender in Orr. They enjoy the lifestyle and typically find a way to make it work. They don't have a retirement plan, and there's no big house or new car. Yet they seem happy and content. They go to their brothers to have their car fixed. Their next-door neighbors may do their electrical work when something breaks down in the home. And they might put off medical care until there is a crisis because the nearest facility is 70 miles down a two-lane road. Overall though, they make it work, surviving.

Way more people in the United States are just surviving than I had thought before starting the trip. Necessity forces them to find solutions. They are resourceful, growing their own food, fixing many things themselves, and making do. It's a growing revelation for me as I ease my way through a second and third beer, talking with the bartender and another buddy who has ambled in after the regulation lunchtime hour.

It's evident in the stories I hear and through personal observation. Once out of the major population areas, I've seen more beat-up cars, boarded-up businesses, people hanging their clothes outside because they probably can't afford a clothes dryer, houses in need of repair. The struggle we all face to survive is more visually evident. From the rural areas of Arkansas, through Oklahoma and Kansas, to the smaller towns of Oregon and Minnesota, I've spoken with farmers and small-town folk who live with a quiet dignity, getting up every morning to take on jobs that barely keep their families above the water line.

It's an eye opener and gives you faith. We all struggle. The challenges people face are all unique. My challenge this summer was making it across the U.S. and Canada. It was a self-imposed challenge, but it also showed that I can survive on a daily basis with very few comfort items. That strengthens my resolve and my belief in our citizens, and what people can still accomplish in the face of hardship. The people I've met living day-to-day have a special zest for life and recognition that a lot of products valued in the material world aren't worth much compared to what's inside the human heart.

***

The sun stuns my eyes when I walk outside the bar. You forget how dark a bar is until you have three beers at 1:30 in the afternoon then step outside to an azure upper-Midwest sky. I breathe deeply through my nose, sucking in the fresh air, glad to be alive and biking.

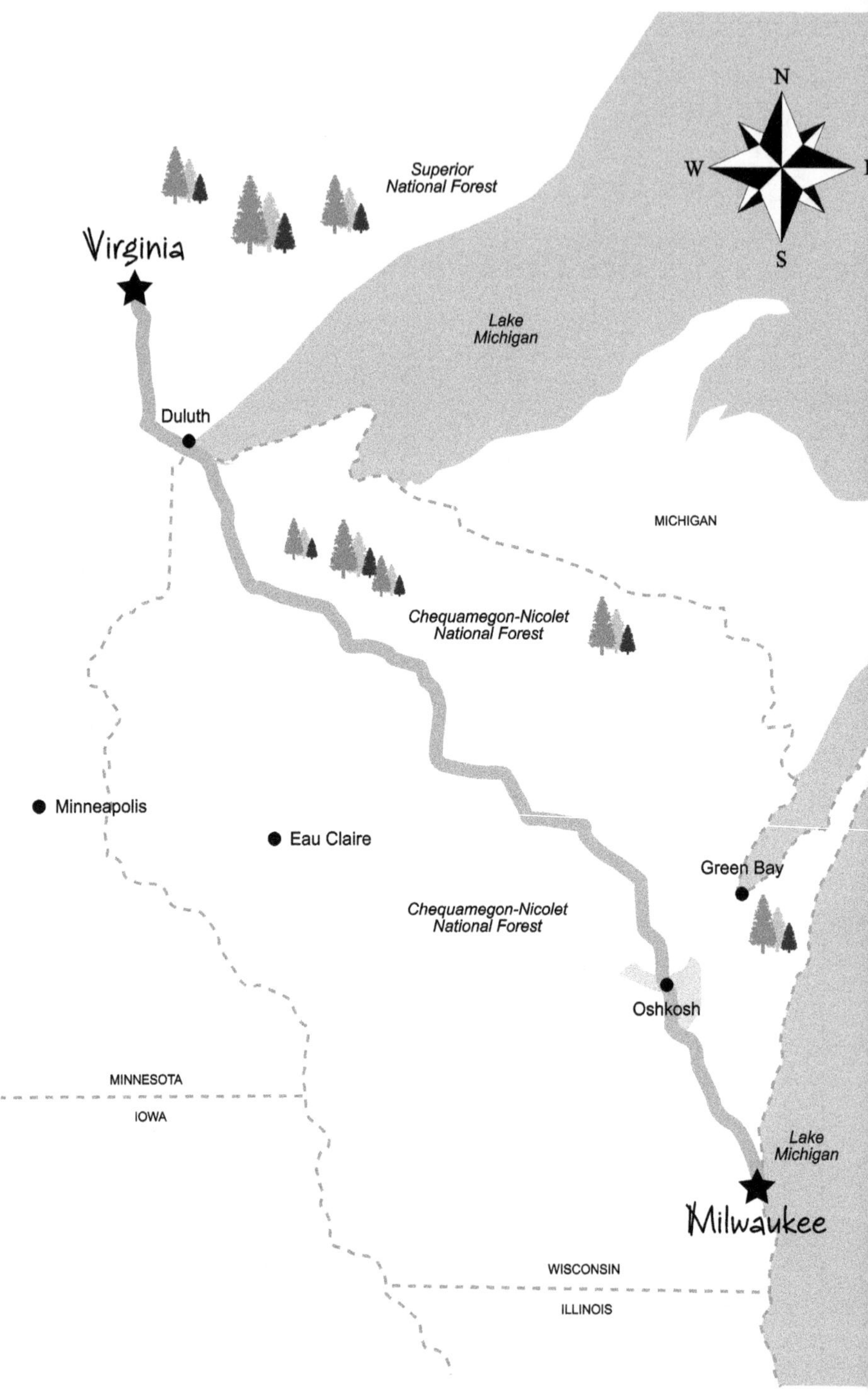
N
W
E
S
Superior
National Forest
Virginia
Lake
Michigan
Duluth
MICHIGAN
Chequamegon-Nicolet
National Forest
Minneapolis
Eau Claire
Green Bay
Chequamegon-Nicolet
National Forest
Oshkosh
MINNESOTA
IOWA
Lake
Michigan
Milwaukee
WISCONSIN
ILLINOIS

Chapter 17
Back in Wisconsin

One thing about biking across North America is that you get a feel for locations, the terrain, the people, attitudes. That feel for Minnesota, which I'm now leaving, was about the outdoor sense of people. They boat, bike, fish. I heard stories of ice fishing in the winter, drinking from flasks, snowmobiling across hard frozen areas in temperatures below zero, cross-country skiing in pristine snow through city parks groomed for that purpose. I passed beautiful golf courses, acres and acres and acres of forest, much of it part of the state or federal system. Canoes being pulled by cars or stashed in the back of trucks were frequently noticeable throughout the ride.

Dropping down into Superior, Wisconsin, from Duluth, I'm struck by the change. This is blue collar territory. You see manufacturing plants, plumes of smoke billowing from their stacks. The road quickly becomes potted and rough. Houses are run down. It's working reality for people in hard factory jobs here. Like each day on the bike trip, every day is a challenge. That's a HUGE part of the U.S. Cars are older, houses a bit more run down. Money is leaking out of this area, and nothing is probably replacing it. Decay occurs.

My itch to get home increases. I'm sore and tired. Motivation wanes. When you start thinking of your end destination, you stop living in the moment, though living in the moment is extremely hard when you're on a bicycle for over 3,500 miles. You live out fantasies. You go back over your life. You sing a lot of songs, inventing lyrics about trees, animals, the environment, the future. Some make sense. I bellow at the top of my lungs to an audience that will never hear my bad voice.

The trip taught me not to get ahead of myself, to stay in the moment. It took well over a thousand miles before I figured that out. Starting out, there was a lot more anticipation and projection to my days: "I hope this happens," or, "I wonder what this state will be like?" Rather than taking it as it came, there was looking ahead to what it "might" be. That's hard to stop doing.

I'm not sure if there was a defining moment in coming to this realization. The recognition developed over time, mostly related to the mileage I piled up daily. "Why do I need to bike so many miles today?" was a question I asked myself that made me take a step back and pay more attention to the daily rhythms. That took time. I think that's another lesson that evolved from the trip: Magical moments are rare. Treasure them. Most of the good things in life evolve over time and take tremendous hard work. Enjoy the moments and stay focused on working towards your goals.

Even as I enter Wisconsin for the final stretch, I battle to stay present. It's challenging because I'm alone with my mind. I have no one to bounce things off or converse with for my entire day on the bicycle. When I stop to buy food and get water, the interchanges bring me back to the moment, which is good. But once I saddle back up and start pedaling, it's me and my imagination, which wants to scatter in many directions, just like the song says, "It was just my imagination once again, running away with me."

Several times over the course of the trip, I've hitched rides with cars or trucks. There are multiple reasons I did this. Often it was convenience. I'd meet someone while watering up, we'd start a conversation, hit it off, and I'd find out the person was going in the same direction and they'd offer to drive me a bit, and I'd accept. But there were also times where I was just plain tired, like heading up Rabbit Ears Pass with Randy. Or frustration hit, like the four flat tires that cold morning in eastern Colorado. It never came down to weather or impending darkness at the end of the day. Ultimately, weather passes, and you get through it. If it got dark, I just found a place to stay off from the road.

I'm a bit behind in terms of getting back to Milwaukee and preparing for the fall semester. Coupled with my general worn-out feel, I decide to stick my thumb out as I start heading east from Osseo to Oshkosh on Route 10. I'm quickly picked up by a doctor driving a stick shift Saab.

He's in a hurry but likes to talk. He wears eggshell glasses and has long blond hair, shaggy and parted on the side so it falls down over his right ear and curls back up. I hop in and swear he's downshifted and got his sports car up to 75 mph in about five seconds. It feels that way. Very weird to be in a vehicle again after so many miles and days on the seat of a bicycle.

Stan is a bicyclist, too. He's taken several lengthy trips and regales me with his tales, pumping me for information on my trip as he shifts down and up again, maneuvering out into the passing lane and flooring it as I try not to choke on the words. He pins me into the seat as he slams the accelerator and revs back into our lane. He wants to be back bicycling but has to attend to his doctor's practice. I sense his impatience and wonder if he's remembering the serenity from his days on the road pedaling. I hope so. It's nice to hear where he's been, but he seems tense and unable to relax. Will this be me in the coming weeks?

He drops me off outside Oshkosh with a wave and peels off to see his patients. Nice guy, but I'm not sure I'd want him operating on me.

***

Traffic slowly increases south of Oshkosh once I'm back on the bike. Almost imperceptibly, I feel the difference. Where once a car would come up from behind once every few minutes, it changes to once a minute, then once every thirty seconds. The intensity rises. My pace quickens. I head towards Lake Michigan to get a final feel for the great outdoors of Wisconsin, this amazing body of water that shapes so much of the area.

I've always thought of the Great Lakes as miniature oceans. As a country, we are blessed with the resource. Living in Milwaukee, the lake shapes culture. Parks dot the waterfront. Beaches are set up to bring swimmers down to enjoy the water.

Bikers, joggers, and people on roller skates regularly populate the area.

As I come down from Bayside, Fox Point, Whitefish Bay, and Shorewood, my pace quickens. The lake shimmers off to the east. The trees canopy above me on North Lake Drive. I'm home. I continue towards the East Side, where I've stored my possessions with the Kuhnen family on Summit Avenue. They agreed to put me up as a boarder upon my return, allowing me a free summer to take on the journey.

August 18, I make it there in the humid air. No one is around when I arrive, but soon enough, Mrs. Kuhnen comes home and runs to hug me.

"I can't believe how skinny you are. You need to eat something," she exclaims.

I've lost 14 pounds on the journey, returning at 179 pounds after starting at 193. I wouldn't recommend this painful weight loss program to anyone, and I know it won't continue once I settle back into my daily routine. Mrs. Kuhnen will make sure of that. As a classic German Catholic mother, she cooks huge meals for the family, with enough to go around and feed more than ten people on any given evening.

I'm confident I'll be eating more than my share in the days and weeks ahead.

I store my bike in the Kuhnen's shed, unsure how soon I will ride again. I feel simultaneously sad and fulfilled. The trip had way more highs and lows than expected: physically and emotionally demanding, painful, lonely, exhilarating, enlightening, challenging.

I started this journey not knowing what to expect. The trip forced me to overcome fears of uncertainty, to engage with strangers, and to deal with physical and emotional challenges I did not anticipate. Riding across this great land and that of our neighbor to the north revealed to me what a vast and diverse treasure of people and natural beauty exist that most will never experience as they grind through the daily business of life. The trip, the journey, the odyssey will stir my soul for the rest of my life. The summer of 1982, that of the cycling nomad.

Shortly after returning to Milwaukee

Epilogue
36 Years Later

Today it's 36 years after the trip. Hard to believe.

People still frequently ask me about it. My older brother Peter, who inspired me to write this book, wanted me to share the stories and insights. I guess that makes much of what occurred timeless.

But there is also a sense of perspective 36 years later. Our country has changed (Canada, too, I'm sure) for good, but it's taken some bad turns as well. The most basic change is population. Our current U.S. population is approximately 325 million. In 1982, it was 231 million. One simple fact: If you did this trip today, the roads would be way more crowded. That's a danger.

The other danger today is distracted driving. It seriously scares me. I bike commuted 13 miles one way for over ten years while living in the Washington, D.C. area, and I never once worried about a distracted driver because smart phones didn't exist then. You had rude drivers, no question, but not people looking down at their laps while pretending to pay attention to the road. That's how bicyclists get hit and killed. I've heard multiple horror stories from seasoned bicyclists since moving back to Wisconsin in August of 2016. These are people who know how to ride properly and protect themselves, and they are scared. So am I.

While living in Texas for 12 years before moving to Wisconsin, I bike commuted again (one to three days a week) for six years. The drivers are more intense there, less biker-friendly, and I had many close calls of people shouting at me and trying to drive me off the road at intersections, stop signs, and stoplights. It's partly an urban issue and partly a crowding issue. People are stressed with traffic. They don't want anyone on the road to slow them down. And they WILL take it out on you. The stories of road rage abound, and bicyclists bear that anger in many circumstances.

After a hiatus where I worked at home for two years, I went back to a corporate job and could have begun bike commuting again. It never entered my mind. The increase in traffic in the two years I'd been working out of the house combined with my more risk-averse age (being two years deeper into my 50s) made me skittish. I felt some car driver would lose it and purposefully knock me down. That's a sad thing to say. All roads should be bicycle-friendly, but I think that is occurring mostly in progressive, forward-thinking communities that put a premium on alternative modes of transportation.

Over these ensuing years, I've been asked many times if I would take the trip again. I've always hedged. The thought occurred to me many times, and I have obsessed over it during certain periods of my life: take our three kids with me when they are old enough to accept the challenge and have my wife meet us along with way with the car, where we'd stay in hotel rooms and use more of today's amenities – laptop, credit cards, real food; have my older brother Peter take a video of my trip and capture the terrain, encounters, and my thoughts along the way; do a shortened version and just cover specific parts of the two countries. There are multiple options. Each one has something going for it, but they also have negatives.

Fundamentally, it would come down to having the time, physical stamina, and desire. You have to want it. That was the drive to take the trip the first time. To do it again, I would need to have similar feelings. It hasn't reached the crescendo, so I continue with all the other activities of my day-to-day life.

It is easy to talk myself out of it. "My body would be in too much pain. I probably can't tolerate an 80- or 120-mile day. The dangers are greater now from increased traffic and distracted drivers. It is too much of a time commitment. I can't get that type of time away from the job." The excuses are endless and really are excuses if I use them to stop a new trip. But that's not the case.

I feel the pull to see the countries with new eyes. How have we changed? Are the people and how they act much different from 1982? How much more built-up are the two countries? The questions go on. The most compelling reason would be a comparison of the two time periods – a then and now descriptive narrative. It might still happen, but at age 62, my window is slowly closing in terms of seriously making plans.

***

As noted earlier in the book, I left with very little money, a map that I changed on a state-by-state basis as I crossed state lines, a pen and notebook to write, a camera, some books to read, basic clothing, and camping and bicycling gear. I cut myself off from the world. Except for that day after the titanic thunderstorm outside Manhattan, Kansas, I didn't read a newspaper. I didn't watch any television news or get updates except when I stayed with friends, relatives, and families I met along the way, and even then I purposefully stayed away from the news. The focus was on the trip, the people, the experiences, and the feelings.

Because of that isolation, I missed out on some things that summer of 1982. There was hype before I debarked from Milwaukee on two summer blockbuster movies: "E.T. the Extraterrestrial" and "Poltergeist." It took years before I finally saw them. I missed a certain essential of the American experience that summer. Both movies captured something in the imagination of the country, and when I returned to daily life in mid-August, popular culture continued to exhort their merits and long-term runs in the theater. Today, with social media and saturation media in general, I doubt you could get away with not having someone bring up a significant event in conversation. Maybe I'm wrong on that count, but people biking cross-country today would certainly have a tougher time completely removing themselves from electronic communication interference. Even if you didn't bring any of the tools with you, every stop would have a TV blaring and just watching people walking into stores tapping away on their phone screens would cause you to wonder what's going on. You'd have to remove your curiosity to ask those bystanders, "Hey, what the heck is going on? Something must be pretty important for you to keep typing away as you go in to buy pork chops. Has someone launched a nuclear missile?"

I'm sure I missed out on many other events that summer, but memory fails to bring back any significant ones. Storing my bike and flying to Houston to see my parents for the family wedding briefly reintroduced me to the big city world, how crowded and pressed for time it is. In the ensuing years, that has only gotten worse. It is one of the most significant issues in our country (massive growth of our megalopolises and the decline of smaller communities) not being addressed by public policy. I fear both types of communities lose – the bigger ones become more costly and crowded as younger people and new businesses move there and the older ones become more run-down and tribal as citizens leave. In the 1950s, Paul Goodman touched on this problem in his writings, arguing for trying to maintain more mid-sized population areas. I think that is the way to go and am heartened in the past few years to see some areas of the country which have been on the losing end of the deindustrialization in the U.S. start to come back with vigor. It's a good thing.

***

I would be remiss if I didn't touch briefly on my love for the bicycle, how important it is to me, and why I think more people should bike – either for exercise, commuting, or just plain fun. I biked to school as a kid, like many other children in the 1960s. The fun, freedom, and increased speed (compared to walking) gave me a strong connection to the bicycle that stayed with me a long time and fueled some of my desire for a cross-country trek.

I bike commuted while working in Washington, D.C., for 13 years, showering at work. The exercise was great. I avoided traffic. I was in control rather than a car or public transportation. I did not have to pay for gasoline. I loved seeing traffic jams and just continuing to pedal and pedal, passing car after car after car, with the people stuck inside fuming while I continued on my merry way. It was a great feeling – continuing to move. And that emotion has stayed with me for years – wanting to keep moving. As my wife will attest, there is nothing that infuriates me more than being stuck in traffic. I become a bad person.

If we could get more people bike commuting, our society would benefit through exercise. Our roads would be less crowded. People would be happier. We'd each be more in control of our own destiny. If you'll indulge me one political rant here, I FIRMLY believe much of the frustration in society today is heavily driven because of events out of our control. We obsess about things we can't do anything about. Car traffic is an example. Yes, you can find new routes, or commute earlier, avoid certain roads, carpool, telecommute, take a bus or train where available, but many of us are still stuck with a short list of options. Biking is a large contributing solution that can both help you on a personal level and a community level. You feel better because of the exercise, you're in control of the movement, you're not paying someone else for the gasoline or electricity to power your vehicle. You take back some degree of control over your life. That's a good thing. Try it. I think many, many people would be way better off physically, psychologically, and emotionally. Our road policies should reflect this awareness and direction. If you care, there are many ways to get involved to build this cultural improvement into your local community or state. It will not happen in a vacuum.

That summer of 1982, I thought long and hard and continuously about the bicycle. After the invention of electricity, the bicycle is the second greatest invention in the history of the world, in my opinion (maybe you need to put the invention of the wheel in the list, too).

Think about it: You can triple your personal speed in getting somewhere using your own power. You just climb on this thing and move your legs. Rather than walking to and from work (how far would you walk to work?), you can now bike 13.5 miles as I did in D.C. You see more. You meet more people. Your awareness is raised. You expand your vision.

Instead of only being able to walk and see friends or to check out some sight, you can increase your mileage almost exponentially. If, for example, you lived in D.C., you could ride to Gettysburg to check out the Civil War grounds. If you had to do that by foot, it would take weeks to get up and back. The point is that your ability to reach out towards the world increases rapidly by hopping on a bike and taking off. That, too, is a good thing.

Finally, on a bike, you are IN the environment. You are not sealed off in a car. That was another motivating variable in taking the trip. I did NOT want to drive a car cross-country. It held no value to me. Anyone could do that. I saw it as the lazy person's way to go. And you are behind a window, blowing through the landscape at 60+ mph. I didn't want that. You don't get a feel for the air, weather, and scenery.

By comparison, riding a bicycle puts you in the countryside. You experience where you are. That sensation is tough to describe but talk to a motorcyclist and he or she will explain it to you – what it's like being in the fresh air, the smells, the weather. The motorcyclist has the negative of going too fast and zooming past sights worth seeing. On a bicycle, you slow down and capture more.

I still ride, and more for fun than for a workout or commuting purposes. The world beckons. It waits to be explored. It could be you out there. Or it could be me. We'll see what the future holds.

Dave Simon started writing for his high school newspaper and never stopped. In addition to his biking expeditions, Dave has journeyed through the written word at multiple stops in his life.

He has self-published two books: 1) *Bad Golf*, a humorous take on why people continue to torture themselves by playing golf, written in an easy-to-read column format, and 2) *Whistle in a Haystack*, with former Division I men's college basketball referee Rick Hartzell. The book chronicles stories from Hartzell's big time basketball officiating career and is loaded with keen life insights and nuggets for any reader. Both are available by contacting Dave through his website at www.justwrite15.com.

In addition to his books, Dave writes a weekly column that has appeared in newspapers in Pennsylvania, Texas, Illinois, and Nebraska since 1998, which he continues to publish on his website. His website also contains a "Bad Golf" blog, a "Meals We Steal" blog, and a weekly chuckle to loosen you up.

Simon began his writing "career" in Washington, D.C., covering environmental issues while reporting on Congress and the Environmental Protection Agency for 10 years.

For 30 years, he has written as a freelancer for *Referee* magazine, a sports officiating publication, and a basketball officiating newsletter put out by the International Association of Approved Basketball Officials.

www.ingramcontent.com/pod-product-compliance
Lightning Source LLC
Chambersburg PA
CBHW061827040426
42447CB00012B/2849

* 9 7 8 1 9 4 8 3 6 5 3 3 8 *